Plant your de
and
Water them g.

Joy

JEMS
FOR
THE
JOURNEY

MEDITATIONS
FOR THE
ADVENTURE OF LIFE

BY

M. JOYCE HALVORSON

Trafford
PUBLISHING

Order this book online at www.trafford.com/08-0537
or email orders@trafford.com

Most Trafford titles are also available at major online book retailers.

Note for Librarians: A cataloguing record for this book is available from Library
and Archives Canada at www.collectionscanada.ca/amicus/index-e.html

Printed in Victoria, BC, Canada.

ISBN: 978-1-4251-6059-3

*We at Trafford believe that it is the responsibility of us all, as both individuals
and corporations, to make choices that are environmentally and socially sound.
You, in turn, are supporting this responsible conduct each time you purchase a
Trafford book, or make use of our publishing services. To find out how you are
helping, please visit www.trafford.com/responsiblepublishing.html*

*Our mission is to efficiently provide the world's finest, most comprehensive
book publishing service, enabling every author to experience success.
To find out how to publish your book, your way, and have it available
worldwide, visit us online at www.trafford.com/10510*

www.trafford.com

North America & international
toll-free: 1 888 232 4444 (USA & Canada)
phone: 250 383 6864 ♦ fax: 250 383 6804 ♦ email: info@trafford.com

The United Kingdom & Europe
phone: +44 (0)1865 487 395 ♦ local rate: 0845 230 9601
facsimile: +44 (0)1865 481 507 ♦ email: info.uk@trafford.com

10 9 8 7 6 5 4 3 2

All scripture quotations have been taken from the following:

The Message: *The Message* by Eugene H. Peterson, copyright (c) 1993, 1994, 1995, 1996, 2000, 2001, 2002. Used by permission of NavPress Publishing Group. All rights reserved.

NIV: Scripture quotations marked (NIV) are taken from the HOLY BIBLE, NEW INTERNATIONAL VERSION®. NIV®. Copyright© 1973, 1978, 1984 by International Bible Society. Used by permission of Zondervan. All rights reserved.

NKJV: Scripture quotations marked "NKJV™" are taken from the New King James Version®. Copyright © 1982 by Thomas Nelson, Inc. Used by permission. All rights reserved.

M. JOYCE HALVORSON

Acknowledgements

I would like to take this opportunity to thank all the people who helped shape this book, and make it a reality. Your continued belief in my abilities kept me going. I owe you all an enormous debt of gratitude. Thank you, thank you, and thank you. There are a few that I would like to mention here:

Living Springs Christian Fellowship in Airdrie, Alberta – Thank you for allowing me to hone my writing skills on the back of the Sunday bulletins.

Marie Cole – You spent countless hours proofreading and offering suggestions. You were invaluable. Thank you for being my second set of eyes.

Pastor Bill Ashbee – former pastor. Thank you for insisting on excellence and for pushing me towards that goal when we first discussed my writing abilities.

Leona Fraser – artist and friend extraordinaire – You gave your time and talent to paint a cover for my book. Thank you so very much.

M. JOYCE HALVORSON

Introduction

Life is a journey. From our birth to the end of our lives we are continually learning, growing and changing. Along the path of life there are potholes that appear to us to be craters, waiting to swallow us whole. Alongside this pathway, we can find treasures that will help us circumvent the craters; while at other times these jewels will open our eyes and help us see that the situations threatening to destroy us are merely potholes after all.

And so it is with this book. It is my hope that each of these "Jems" will encourage, inspire, and provoke you, the reader, to examine your own life and improve the quality of your life's journey. These readings were originally written over several years for my church bulletin. Some of the jems will have sharp edges that spur us on while others will provide comfort through a difficult day. All provide a thoughtful, yet unique look at our needs as fellow travelers.

It is my hope and prayer that your life will become rich with meaning as each thought provoking jem is allowed a place in your life.

JEMS FOR THE JOURNEY

Contents

DARE TO BE DIFFERENT   93

M. JOYCE HALVORSON

RELATIONSHIPS

M. JOYCE HALVORSON

Accountability partners

"Who is wise and understanding among you? Let him show it by his good life, by deeds done in the humility that comes from wisdom."
(James 3:13, NIV)

A dictionary definition of accountable is: "liable to be called to account; answerable". An accountability partner would be someone who understands growth and the Holy Spirit. That one person is in a position of trust in our lives and must be lead by the Holy Spirit. With this person we would share openly and honestly about our fears and failures, struggles and successes. They would be encouraged to hold us accountable. True accountability partnering goes beyond complaining to a friend, and it goes beyond praying together. This person would know us intimately, seeing the minute details of our lives. Our accountability partner would have permission to question what we do and why. When we've shared with them a goal, they need to remind us of that goal. They have been given the responsibility to check up on us and to challenge us should we go astray.

Accountability partnering is not an easy matter. It requires love and patience from both parties involved in the relationship. Pride has no place in this sort of relationship. It requires a deep commitment to humility and godly living. So often today we want to please God. Yet, we insist on doing it our own way.

Or we want to learn new disciplines, but it must be according to the plan we have made. This is not the case in accountability partnering. We may be challenged to face our problems and change. This is not pleasant, tidy work. It is often messy and very painful. However, the end results are worth the pain.

Why all the fuss about accountability? We are made in a relationship. We are healed in a relationship, and we will grow in a relationship. God did not make individuals to stand alone. He intends for us to depend upon each other, not just in the good times, but also in those times when we need to be cared for. While it is true that we are ultimately accountable to God, we must also be accountable to someone whom we trust to tell the truth, no matter how painful it may be for us. We need one person upon whom we can rely for support, encouragement, and honesty.

M. JOYCE HALVORSON

After the party

*"All of us have become like one who is
unclean, and all our righteous acts are like
filthy rags ..."*
(Isaiah 64:6, NIV)

In Luke 15 we are given the account of the prodigal son. The younger of two sons, he demanded his inheritance and then squandered it. The passage tells us that he came to his senses, decided to go home, and throw himself on his father's mercy. Papa saw him coming and treated him royally. The elder brother was quite upset by the party their father put on for his brother and refused to participate.

We are not told what happened after the party, but are left to write our own ending. Did the elder brother choose to ignore his little brother? Was there a rift in the family because of this? Did big brother alienate himself from the rest of the household and surround himself with those sympathetic to his cause? It would be silly, if this were the case. Everything his father had was now his. Little brother had spent his portion of the inheritance and had nothing left.

There is another ending to this story, however. The elder brother was at first upset, and doesn't attend the party. Later on, he examines his heart and understands that he has more than enough and shares what he has with his brother.

He had come to an understanding of his own filthiness and repents. For a while the relationship is strained but with time and some hard work on the part of both brothers and their father, wounds are healed and the severed relationship is mended.

I like happy endings. There is room for hope, healing, and restoration, repentance, and change. It took courage on the elder brother's part to admit to anyone that he was wrong. But he didn't let pride and self righteousness stand in the way. He saw the error of his ways and repented. It didn't stop there. The work continued on. With courage he faced himself, his brother, and their father. Together the difficulties were worked out.

So often we are like the elder brother. We become upset when things don't go the way we think they should. Yet, we have a choice. We can write whatever ending we choose. Do we harbour resentment and bitterness, or will we choose the path to healing and restoration?

Either way, the choice is ours.

M. JOYCE HALVORSON

He's watching the driveway!

"For the eyes of the Lord run to and fro throughout the whole earth, to shew himself strong in the behalf of those whose heart is perfect toward him. . ."
(*2 Chronicles 16:9 KJV*)

Our Father is watching the driveway. When He sees us coming, He flies out of His house and waits with arms open wide. As we come nearer, He moves towards us, wrapping us in His arms. He is more than willing to lavish His love on us. He knows us very well and gives us as much as we can handle at any given time. But we must make the first move. We need to be actively involved in the renewal of our minds. We cannot just sit down and expect God to transform us. It is also true that God is waiting for us to come to Him. It's almost like the prodigal son returning home. If you're like me and you've tried everything from quoting the Word to being stubborn and falling and falling and . . . pray this prayer with me:

God, I've tried so hard! I've done all the things I'm supposed to do like reading your Word, and looking for truth in a situation. I've even been confessing your word audibly. I've ignored how I feel and pushed myself out of my comfort zone. Nothing is working. I cannot change me. I believe what you said in the Bible is true. I come to you with all my imperfections and faults. I know you will not turn me away. I do not need to become better for you to allow me into your throne room.

God, you are looking for people just like me who want you more than anything else. You will not reject me because of my imperfections. You already love me just the way I am. My heart is firmly set toward you, Father. I want to know you more. Change the way I think. Pour into my mind your thoughts so that incorrect thoughts are drowned out and washed away. Show me those areas of my live that you want me to change, what I read and see and do. I know I cannot do it on my own. I give up, God! I need help! Change me! Transform me into your image.

Remove those grave clothes

> *"Take off the grave clothes and let him go."*
> (John 11: 44, NIV)

The story is told of Lazarus, Jesus' friend. He was very sick and subsequently died. In those days they wrapped the deceased in strips of cloth, much like the Egyptian mummies. The cloths went round and round until the entire body was covered. It was into this situation that Jesus arrived – three days after Lazarus's body had been wrapped and placed in a tomb. The story continues with Martha confronting Jesus upon His arrival. *"Lord,"* Martha said to Jesus,

> *"if you had been here, my brother would not have died. . ."*
>
> (John 11:21, NIV)

Jesus informs her that Lazarus will live again and eventually He goes to the tomb. He asks for the stone to be removed and then orders Lazarus to come out of that tomb. To the astonishment of all those around, Lazarus appears. But there is a problem. Lazarus is still all bound up and completely encircled by the grave clothes of that day. Jesus took one look at him and said to remove the rags that held him captive.

Was Jesus not capable of unwinding those strips of cloth? Of course he was. He was as human as anyone there. He was able to do it. Yet, he said for the people around him to do it. The same is true for us today.

We intercede for the needs around us, and then rejoice when there is an answer to prayer. However, we often wonder at the difficulty people have when they have received an answer to prayer or when the Holy Spirit has come into their lives in a new way. What has transpired is that someone has been brought to life; but they are still carrying the grave clothes wound tightly around them. Those same people are incapable of unwinding those confining strips on their own and depend upon people around them to loose them and let them go. This is a responsibility that can take a great deal of time. Yet, it is ours to do. Jesus is calling us, "Loose them and let them go. Don't hang onto what is not yours, and please don't force someone to act a certain way. Remove the constrictions and hindrances. Get busy, now. Loose them. Unwind the grave clothes."

Let's start now. Let's get rid of the restricting and confining rags. Let's loose them and let them go!

M. JOYCE HALVORSON

The face cloth

"For now we see through a glass darkly; but
then face to face..."
(I Corinthians 13:12)

I've had pink eye and for part of the time it felt as though there was fog everywhere. I was definitely not seeing very clearly. Whatever was in my eyes was preventing clear vision. Then I started thinking about Lazarus after Jesus ordered him out of the tomb. He'd been dead for several days and completely encased in strips of cloth – burial clothes. Jesus told the people around him to remove the grave clothes. Lazarus was alive, but all bound up; and the family and friends were expected to loose him and let him go. I am sure the first item that was removed was the face cloth because this was preventing him from seeing at all; it was impeding his vision.

Jesus wanted Lazarus to be able to function normally without any hindrances. In the same way the people in Jesus' day were instructed to remove the face cloth, so are we today expected to remove whatever is hindering people from seeing clearly.

Sometimes we grow accustomed to doing things a certain way, and insist that everyone do them that way as well; or we fail to admit our own shortcomings and instead criticize other people. This can only bring confusion to people who are struggling with their new life. It shifts the focus from new growth to isolation and defensiveness. This kind of attitude teaches people watching us to be wary and creates difficulties where there doesn't need to be any. This is not at all pleasing to God. He wants us to be open and honest with each other.

I am told that pink eye sometimes causes the eye to be stuck shut when we wake up. When this occurs the eyes need to be gently cleaned with a warm cloth. In the same way, we must have patience with each other. Where there is confusion and blurred vision we are to soak that person in love and gentleness. The crustiness so frequently in evidence can be changed into freedom as the scales are gently soaked away.

Just like my eyes needed medication to enable them to see more clearly, so we must medicate the eyes of those who are having difficulty in their vision. Let's begin today to remove those unnecessary face cloths.

Let me hear!

". . . work out your own salvation . . . for it
is God who works in you to will and to act
according to his good purpose."
(Philippians 2:12 & 13)

Jesus had done His work. Now he depended upon the people around Lazarus do unwind the grave clothes. First the face cloth was removed. Lazarus could see once again! He may have blinked as the sun shone on his face once again! He looked around and saw . . . Jesus – his best friend, and his family! The cloth wrapped around his head was then removed. His ears were uncovered as those closest to him reversed the burial process. I wonder if he heard the birds singing that day as the people stood in awe of what they'd witnessed. The same is true for us as Christians, both for the Lazarus's and for those around the Lazarus's.

God has done incredible things in a person's life. Yet, old habits and unnecessary advice are cluttering their hearing. These people are still struggling with wrong patterns of behavior. It's not that

God hasn't answered prayer; it's just that they need to learn new responses and new behavior patterns. This takes time and the help and support of caring people. We begin rolling away the burial clothes around their heads when we give positive support and encouragement. Offering encouragement empowers the recipient to hear what God is saying to him/her. It builds their confidence that what they are hearing is accurate.

For the "Lazarus's", it is vital to choose whom you will confide in and who your counselors are. Going to several people for advice and counsel can hinder your hearing. It confuses rather than clarifies.

It would be really nice if we could sit down and wait for people around us to do all the work. But that is not what is intended. Jesus said to loose Lazarus and let him go. He meant for the people to free him to do, and go, and be. It takes hard work; failure is guaranteed, but it is only temporary. Once we have fallen, we stand up and try again.

Whether we are a Lazarus or one of those already walking in freedom, we have a job to do. Jesus is calling each of us, "loose him and let him go". It is our responsibility to facilitate freedom in those around us.

From the inside out

"Take off the grave clothes and let him go."
(John 11: 44, NIV)

I fried my thumb so badly that I thought I would permanently lose sensation and thumb print. That, of course, turned out to be exaggerated. The back of my thumb was numb for a few weeks. One day I noticed some loose skin – my thumb had healed from the inside out, and now the outer layer of skin was being sloughed off.

Healing from the inside out takes a long time; we would not see any difference if we looked in the mirror. A lasting change, the kind that begins on the inside is not a visible change. It is true that changes are taking place, but we cannot see them. People around us may not be aware that God is doing anything at all in our lives. Yet, we are in agony as our lives are being changed and rearranged by the Holy Spirit. It is a private work of the Holy Spirit and will only be visible to those around us when the work is almost complete. We want to be more like Jesus, and then go about making what we think are the necessary changes. Unfortunately, we can only work on the outside; lasting change always begins on the inside.

The Holy Spirit requires our co-operation with change, but the actual work of renovation is His responsibility. True change will start when we begin to honestly ask God to change the sin patterns that keep our hearts dirty. Just like King David we need to ask God to change us from the inside out.

It is equally important to remember that God is doing a deep work in our hearts. It's a private work; and it is between each of us (individually) and God. We may not even be aware of the change as it takes place in our own lives, but God can be relied upon to complete the work that has begun within each of us.

Just like the healing that took place in my thumb, so is the healing that takes place whenever we pray for our lives to change; it's a gradual work, and not instant. Let's begin today to co-operate with the Holy Spirit as he begins the work deep within. Change me, God, on the inside!

Butterflies

*". . . he who began a good work in you will
carry it on to completion until the day of
Christ Jesus."*
(Philippians 1:6, NIV)

There are four stages in the life of the butterfly: egg, larvae or caterpillar, pupa, and adult. Each stage is significant, and each stage has its characteristics. I am sure that if these tiny creatures could talk, they would exult over each stage as if they had already arrived at maturity. The most frustrating stage is that of the pupa. As a caterpillar, the butterfly could at least inch along. Life may have been slow, but it was life at its best. As a pupa, the poor butterfly cannot move at all. It once knew the joy of freedom and movement. But now it appears that all is lost. There is no productivity, and no action. Life has seemingly ground to a halt. What does not appear are the changes now in progress within the tiny creature. While in an inactive state, the most work is going on inside the caterpillar. There is no point in fighting, because it is helpless. The continual eating has stopped, and it now appears lifeless. Soon, however, a new creature emerges. It is an incredibly beautiful butterfly. Just like a butterfly, we become a new creation when we accept Christ as Saviour.

Someone somewhere planted a seed that took on life as the Holy Spirit breathed into it. Soon, a new creation emerged. We were delighted with our new life. It was good to be alive. Never noticing that life was slow, we exulted in each new day, and fed continually on the life giving Word of God. Suddenly, something changed. We could no longer move around, and we began to complain. We could not understand why God would suddenly desert us. However, just like the caterpillar experiencing change deep within him, so we are experiencing growth and change deep within us. Life has not ground to a halt; life has continued.

It is at this stage of our growth as Christians that we are most often tempted to complain. "God has forsaken us," we often cry. All the while God is at work in us, perfecting us. Now is not the time to complain. It is time to rest. We will emerge as a beautiful new creation -- in His time.

Coulda, shoulda, woulda

*"God isn't so easily diverted. He sees right
through all smoke screens and holds you
to what you've done. You didn't think, did
you, that justly pointing your finger at
others you would distract God from coming
down on you hard. . . God is kind, but he's
not soft. In kindness he takes us firmly by
the hand and leads us into a radical life
change."*
(Romans 2:2-4, The Message)

I've been thinking about taking some computer courses. I know
I should do this because it will bring me up to industry standard
in my career. I really should pick a computer school and make an
appointment. I should call a friend. I should get busy and write
that article. I should spend more time with the Lord. I woulda
done more for God had I the resources. I coulda done better, but
he wouldn't let me.

"Shoulda's, woulda's, and coulda's" keep us well within the confines of our comfort zones. "If we make a move to do anything different from what we've done in the past and it doesn't work out, we are failures" is the excuse we use for not trying. Then we continue the self-effacing diatribe of, "I'm not good enough. I will never amount to anything. It was their fault, not mine", and so on. Our complaints keep us within the protective barriers that we've erected between ourselves and the outside world." Sadly enough, they also keep us insulated from God and all that He wants to do in our lives.

As long as we can point our finger at another's imperfections, then no one will notice our own—right? Wrong!! We may think we are protecting ourselves from further pain and disillusionment when we point out imperfections in others, but all we are really doing is reinforcing that horrible wall of protection around our own hearts and lives. Our faulty thinking tells us that we are protected because no one will be able to see, or pay attention to, our imperfections. They will be too busy looking at everyone else. That may be partly true.

I'm glad God is not so easily distracted. He sees right through us. We have a choice. We can choose to remain in our misery or we can choose to let go and let God lead us into an incredible life.

M. JOYCE HALVORSON

Changes

*"For if you live according to the sinful
nature, you will die; but if by the Spirit you
put to death the misdeeds of the body, you
will live,"*
(Romans 8:13, NIV)

Changes are hard work. It's much easier to remain in an old pattern of thinking or living than to do something different. We have talked about blaming others for our indecisiveness. We said that it is easier to look at the imperfections in other people than to deal with our own. It makes us feel better, and we are able to deceive ourselves into thinking we are better than we really are. God sees right through the self deception. He is waiting to lead us into an abundant life as we allow Him access into our lives.

When we pray for God to do a deep work in our lives, we are inviting Him to shine his search light into every area, showing us those things we need to work on. I can remember many people whose lives appeared to be changed in a moment upon meeting with God. Those same people fought for years to bring into obedience their old way of living. The adage, old habits die hard, proved to be true in their lives. Sometimes we're determined to make a change; other times the Holy Spirit gives us a nudge, drawing us into greater intimacy. No one said it would be easy; the opposite most often is true.

Change begins with taking a look at all the shoulda's in our lives. Write them down in a column. Beside each, write a possible action that you can take towards destroying that pattern of behavior or thought. Include scripture to support what you intend to do. At first it may seem like it's only baby steps that you've taken. You may be tempted to quit, thinking that God has not lead you in this area. Don't quit! Sometimes lives are instantly changed, while in other cases, it takes persistent, concentrated effort to effect the desired change.

The choice is ours. As we reach out to Him, He will take us by the hand and walk with us all the way. The way may be difficult and the path strewn with debris, but the journey we embark upon is well worth the continued exertion. As we learn obedience, we will grow into amazing men and women of God.

Claustrophobia

*"I will be glad and rejoice in your love, for
you saw my affliction and knew the anguish
of my soul. You have not handed me over
to the enemy but have set my feet in a
spacious place"*
(Psalm 31:7 & 8, NIV)

I like my space; just ask anyone who works with me. The unit work space is designed in such a way that it tends to collect far more people than should be there. I cannot work with people crowding around me. This is exactly how I feel when life's problems and challenges crowd my space. It would be nice if we could schedule appointments for life's challenges and take one at a time, but that's not life! This tends to occur on a regular basis and I want to run away and hide. Sometimes I wish for a hole to open up so that I can jump in and pull the opening in after me!

In our verse for today, David declares that God knows all about the afflictions and torment he has been forced to endure. But He wasn't left there to face the enemy on his own! It was not in his own strength that he lived. God took David and put him in a place where he could move. He had breathing space; he would not be cramped or crowded by the stress of all he faced.

This is exactly what God does for us. There is no need to run away. He removes us from the dismal overcrowded places we find ourselves in. The sheer magnitude of having space causes our spirits to relax and find that place of peace and rest. God cares, and knowing those two words reminds us of where we must start. Talk to Him; pour out your despair and frustration. He will listen. The problems will be there, but the stress they've caused will be dissolved. We will then be able to effectively deal with them, because we have God on our side.

The problems of life tend to crowd in around us and weigh us down, causing the panic of claustrophobia. God wants to set us in a place where we can move about freely and be able to breathe. We are His children; He is our Father. He has the answer to our problems. Let's ask Him.

Feelings

Finally, brethren, whatsoever things are
true, whatsoever things are honest . . . think
on these things.
(Philippians 4:8, KJV)

God made us, and He put within us our emotions and the capacity to feel. He gave us the ability to experience heat and pain when we touch a hot stove, or like myself, a hot curling iron. We have the delightful ability to experience cold when we have an ice cream cone during extreme heat. These feelings are essential to our well being. Lepers, for example, cannot experience heat and pain in the same way, and as a result they can be seriously injured. People with poor peripheral circulation often develop open sores on their feet because they cannot experience discomfort the way healthy people do.

In much the same way we experience emotions. The ability to experience emotions was placed within us by God and is essential to our well being. When my father encountered difficulty during his aborted mission trip, the entire family experienced anxiety in varying degrees. It was important for us to acknowledge the emotion before we could take it to the Lord who is the God of all comfort.

We must also allow ourselves to admit to feelings of anger, frustration, joy, and sadness; and a host of others as well. It is in doing so that we can come before God with an honest heart asking Him to help us deal with what we are experiencing. It is seldom useful to deny our true feelings. It is more correct to confess them and then take those feelings to God.

When we consider Philippians 4, we are honestly acknowledging how we feel. Then we take those feelings and emotions to God in prayer. Frequently, when we have failed to admit to experiencing what we perceive to be negative, we have failed to be honest, not only with ourselves but also with God. The continual stuffing down of our emotions prevents healing from taking place. It is essential that we allow the wound to open so that the Holy Spirit can pour in the oil and the wine and rid us of infection (sin) that will continue to grow unless removed.

Why are we angry, or sad, or glad? God will give us the answer as we humble ourselves before him. The result?

> "Whatever you have learned or received or heard from me, or seen in me—put it into practice. And the God of peace will be with you."

(Philippians 4:9, NIV)

M. JOYCE HALVORSON

I need you!

"Do not conform any longer to the pattern of this world, but be transformed by the renewing of your mind. "
(Romans 12:2, NIV)

I wanted to write something new and fresh, so I've been looking through my files. I guess you could say that I've been renewing my memory. There are all kinds of good thoughts and ideas in my files. No doubt they were inspired by the Holy Spirit. One thing stands out to me regarding much of what I looked through, and that is the importance of relationships, and how much we need each other. God made us to be relational beings.

When we pray for the renewal of our minds, we need others to pray with us and for us because of the authority there is in united prayer. Our minds and spirits must recognize the authority of another's prayers. It helps us to disengage from wrong thinking and to begin to develop an inner dialogue of truth.

God has uniquely gifted each one of us. We are all different, and we must accept our own uniqueness as well as accepting others just the way they are. Other scriptures remind us that

"iron sharpens iron" (Proverbs 27:17, NIV)

and *"speak the truth in love."* (Ephesians 4:15, NIV)

Each of us tend to see the same situation differently, and it is these differing viewpoints that give us a clearer idea of what the big picture is. We have limited understanding in so many areas of life. That's where friends and family come in. We may think we have a clear view of what we should do, but when we've heard from a few trusted advisers, the situation suddenly takes on a different hue. It is true that we do hear, individually, from God. But it is equally true that our friends help us to see what we may fail to see or do not wish to see. They help us to hear another point of view, which could reinforce what we feel God wants us to do. It also helps to solidify our own thoughts and dreams. Another's prayers frequently bring into focus those areas of our lives that are hindering us from significant growth. All this occurs when we are in the relationships God designed for us, and it is in such relationships that we begin our journey to the renewal of our minds.

M. JOYCE HALVORSON

Infectious diseases

"The joy of the Lord is your strength."
(Nehemiah 8:10, NIV)

I work in a hospital. There are all kinds of bugs and viruses that tend to attack a patient's body. Whenever a patient is known to have certain "bugs" in their system, we place that patient in a private room and follow isolation procedures, protecting him/her and staff alike. Bugs are contagious, as are some diseases. A dictionary defines contagious as, caught or communicated by contact, infectious. We have an entire department in the hospital that is devoted to infection prevention and control. They ensure that correct policy and procedures are followed; their doctors are frequently consulted when an infection cannot be eradicated by usual antibiotics. Of course, we have no wish to become infected by any of these dread diseases so we do our best to prevent their spread. There is, however, one disease I love to spread.

The Israelites had been working incredibly hard restoring their towns and cities. They'd been in captivity for years and now they'd returned home, despite opposition. It had been brutally hard work, and they were tired. They wept as they heard the Word of the Lord read to them. They were reminded that God had returned them; they were instructed not to grieve, but to rejoice because the joy of the Lord was their strength!

A smile or comment given to a fellow staff member or patient can change their outlook on life – at least for a moment or two. That moment or two may make a huge difference in their lives. I have also noticed the opposite: when a negative comment is uttered by someone, the person hearing the comment becomes negative as well. When work has been especially stressful, some of us have a tendency to tell jokes or repeat funny anecdotes, and laughter results. The end result is a lighter atmosphere.

Joy, true joy, is contagious. Whenever we are thankful and allow ourselves to be vocal about it, joy becomes infectious. We cannot change our past; we can only improve the present and future. It is time to stop the mourning over our past failures, be glad that God is on the throne, and count our many blessings. We are a blessed people! Let's begin today to spread the "infection".

In step with God

> "But by shifting our focus from what we do, to what God does, don't we cancel out all our careful keeping of the rules and ways God commanded? Not at all. What happens, in fact, is that by putting that entire way of life in its proper place, we confirm it."
> (Romans 3:31, The Message)

Some of the Jews in the early church were insisting that non Jewish believers be circumcised in order to truly belong to the church. Paul scolds them for this, insisting that it is not the rules and rituals that save them, but rather faith in God. The Jewish Christians were still so intent on keeping all the rules in addition to their faith that they'd lost the proper perspective. Paul did not suggest that rules were meaningless. He did say that when everything is put in its proper place, what they do carries greater meaning.

Throughout the years since then, there has been resistance to any new work of the Holy Spirit. People have become set in their ways and refused to do anything differently. Each new work of the Holy Spirit was met with resistance by the established church. Anything that could not be readily understood has been rejected. After all, is the argument, God moved when we did this or that, and so it must stay this way. Recognizable patterns are the only way to go.

No doubt the biggest fear most church leaders have with what God is doing today, is that the only pattern is unpredictability. One service can be very quiet and the next very noisy. Frequently altars are full during the worship times. Isn't that supposed to happen after the sermon? But then again sometimes there is no sermon!

We do not need to fear an imbalance in our lives. What we need to do is pray that the leaders in our church will hear the voice of God and instantly obey. When following an unpredictable God, that can be difficult. The second thing we need to pray is that we will follow just as quickly. As we learn obedience to the Holy Spirit's leading we will be able to minister to those who are hurting and lost. Our rituals, those things we do repetitively, will carry greater meaning. They will become symbols of something much more valuable. It is at that moment that all our needs will be met.

Intimacy with God

"Come near to God and he will come near to you."
(James 4:8, NIV)

A little girl was sitting on her daddy's lap. Her daddy has allowed something to happen and now she is very angry. She is kicking and screaming and is trying to turn around. When she manages to manoeuvre around, she shakes her fist in daddy's face and says, "Let me go! I don't love you anymore! I don't want to talk to you!" The harder she kicks and screams, the tighter daddy holds her. He says to her, "I love you. I will never, never let you go."

In the story, "Loved", on page 37 I have used this story to illustrate God the Father's love for his children. There's another side to this story, that of intimacy. If the little girl hadn't enjoyed a close relationship with her father, she would not have been on her father's lap. Neither would she have been in a position to shake her fist in her father's face. She'd spent time with him, sharing her most private thoughts. When something hurt her, she was able to verbalize her anger.

Intimacy begins with spending time with someone, and enjoying conversation with them. Intimacy also implies knowing a person thoroughly, both inside and out. It has reached its full potential when I am free and honest enough with that person to be able to voice my displeasure. Intimacy also implies secrecy, private thoughts, and sharing confidential information.

Intimacy with God is the same way. He is waiting for us to get closer to Him so He can tell us what is on His heart. God longs for us to be honest with Him and tell Him what is on our hearts. Are we happy, sad, contented, or upset? Intimacy with God means sharing my innermost thoughts and His sharing with me. The awesome difference is that intimacy with God will never come to an end. He will not lose patience with us because He loves us with an everlasting love.

Just like the father in our story, our Heavenly Father is waiting for us to come to Him. He wants us to be so close, so intimate, that we can hear His heart beat as he holds us close. He is waiting to whisper in our ears those things intended only for us to hear.

Jesus and I

"Whether you turn to the right or to the left, your ears will hear a voice behind you saying, 'This is the way; walk in it'"
(Isaiah 30:21, NIV)

I have a picture of someone standing at the controls of a ship. There is a storm raging and it is almost impossible to move the steering wheel. The wind is so loud that he cannot hear anyone whispering into his ear. Yet, he is still doing what he knows to do, is calm, and has not run for cover in a panic. I can feel the storm raging whenever I look at the picture. Did I say that Jesus is standing behind the captain? Well, he is and that makes all the difference because His voice can be heard in the most difficult circumstances

I have heard God speak, and some of the time, I have already been planning a course of action. I set my thoughts aside and just am quiet. In my heart I ask God to speak to me, and then I quit talking. That's the easy part! The rest is very hard, but well worth the effort. Our spirits need to slow down as well. It's intimidating to be absolutely quiet—it's terrifying, and for me it is hard because I've heard so many times that I must be independent and should not call anyone else for help. I should be able to fix my own problems. That's quite a dilemma! Most of the time I find that, yes, I do need to problem solve; but while I am formulating a plan of action, I hear God speak. Together God and I are a team. He is the true captain and I am his flunky, blessed beyond belief. I know that no matter what the situation, there is someone bigger than I am that is captain of my ship.

I cannot do it alone;
the waves run fast and high,
and the fogs close all around,
the light goes out in the sky;
but I know that we two shall win in the end,
Jesus and I.
I could not guide it myself,
my boat on life's wild sea;
there's one who sits by my side,
who pulls and steers with me.
And I know that we two shall safe enter port,
Jesus and I.

(Not Alone—author unknown)

M. JOYCE HALVORSON

Loved

"Never will I leave you; never will I forsake you."
(Hebrews 13:5, NIV)

A little girl was sitting on her daddy's lap. Her daddy has allowed something to happen and now she is very angry. She is kicking and screaming and is trying to turn around. When she manages to manoeuvre around, she shakes her fist in daddy's face and says, "Let me go! I don't love you anymore! I don't want to talk to you!" The harder she kicks and screams, the tighter daddy holds her. He says to her, "I love you. I will never, never let you go."

Often we are just like this little girl. Once we enjoyed being God's children. We loved Him and trusted Him implicitly. We felt very secure in God's love for us. We drew strength from Him. Then, something beyond our comprehension happens. Maybe it's an illness in our body or that of a loved one. Perhaps we lose our source of income, or we are treated unfairly. Our confidence in God is shattered. Where is the love we once thought we felt?

Where are the security and protection we understood was ours? How could we have been so hurt? How could the illness or tragedy have happened if our God really was a loving God? We become angry and shake our fist at God, "You blew it!" we scream over and over again.

All during this angry tirade, our Heavenly Father is holding us close. He is fully aware that we do not understand. His Word has made some strong promises. We have believed that these promises will come to pass, and they haven't happened according to our interpretation of scripture. We may not even understand why we feel the way we do, but God does. He created us the way we are, complete with our emotions. He is not upset or offended that we dare to question His behaviour. He loves us, and wants the very best for us. He will never let us go. He holds us close.

Just like a parent holding a hurting child and knowing that the crying will soon stop, He holds us. That child may never understand the trauma inflicted upon him, and so we may not completely understand. The pain will subside; the weeping will stop; the anger will fade. We will find ourselves resting in the strong, gentle arms of the only One who could love us so completely.

Bruises

"A bruised reed he will not break, and a
smoldering wick he will not snuff out."
(Matthew 12:20, NIV)

I'd planted 15 tomato plants one summer. All were growing. I eagerly anticipated a wonderful harvest at summer's end. The weather was great that Saturday. My husband and I took our boys shopping. In our absence a hailstorm came through that part of the city. When we returned, our yard had the appearance of a battlefield. Leaves were strewn about the grass. Those tomato plants had nothing left on them but the main stem! Not much hope for any fresh tomatoes! We cleaned up as best we could, leaving the plants alone.

We are like those bruised and battered tomato plants. Once we were growing, our roots going deep, drawing nurture from the soil. We become beaten by circumstances, or the cruel wounding of someone we know. It was so unexpected. We were ravaged by the hail beating upon us. Our foliage is gone, cruelly torn from its source of life. Any promise of fruitfulness has been destroyed. Our roots remain. Yet what good is a root system when everything above ground appears ruined? It wasn't so long ago that we once held promise. We were a light in a dark place, a beacon set on a hill. Then the strong winds came and we were bent, weakened by the storm, and crushed by the cruelty of life. It's as though our life is over.

The above verse tells us that God will not utterly destroy those who are bruised. He will not completely cut them off. Society tends to ignore the wounded among them. Yet, God will not destroy them. He has promised to rebuild, to heal and to restore; and He accomplishes His work through each of us. Gently, but firmly, the bruised and broken person must be helped. A tender touch, a kind word, a helping hand. All are essential in aiding the restoration of those who have been wounded.

The same holds true for those who are like the smouldering wick. While not quite out, neither is it a flame. God will fan the smouldering and gets it burning brightly once again, restoring it to more than its former usefulness. As for my tomato plants . . . they came back better than ever, producing the best crop of tomatoes I've ever had!

M. JOYCE HALVORSON

Weeds

"The one who sows to please his sinful nature, from that nature will reap destruction; the one who sows to please the Spirit, from the Spirit will reap eternal life."
(Galatians 6:8, NIV)

Eight years ago I'd decided to sell my mobile home. Particularly anxious for my home to have great "curb appeal" I planted some seeds hoping to have a multitude of flowers in my front yard. Spring turned into summer and alas! My flowers never materialized! Somehow I had planted weeds! The packets of marigold seeds were confused with weed seeds. My sister took one look at my "flowers" and promptly declared them weeds! I refused to give up hope and faithfully watered and weeded my plants. Eventually, I capitulated and pulled up what was planted in good faith and with a lot of hope and anticipation.

Regardless of my good intentions, I'd managed to plant weeds with the end result being destruction. The same holds true for our walk with God. If we fail to consult the "owner's manual", the Bible, we will plant weeds that could quite likely poison us. I've watched many gardeners consult books and manuals in an effort to determine what will grow best in their soil. They may like some plants but, upon careful examination will discover those plants to be inappropriate. It takes discipline to plant what is best and not just our favorite plants. The same holds true for us. God has given us the guidelines in His Word that will cause us to grow into mature Christians.

It takes discipline and a lot of work. But the results are well worth the effort. When we discipline our bodies, our minds, and our spirits to become more like Jesus, we will become trees of righteousness, and not weeds. We must carefully examine each thought and each action to determine whether it will help, or hinder, our walk with God. Sometimes, like my would-be flowers, we need to back track and redo some things. I had to pull up those plants that were undesirable, and so we must pull up and destroy all those things in our lives that do not please the Spirit of God. It is only as we remain single minded in our pursuit of righteousness that we will be all that God has ordained that we would be.

Crazy days of summer

". . . seed sown on good soil, hear the word,
accept it, and produce a crop – thirty, sixty
or even a hundred times what was sown."
(Mark 4:20, NIV)

I have spent countless hours in my yard, renovating and rearranging. A great deal of energy and time was involved in preparing the ground to receive the flowers I'd chosen. Without the assistance of a neighbor who'd decided I needed help, I would probably need the entire summer to finish the project. My neighbor started digging up my dirt. Then she asked me what I was planting and where; I helped, of course. Despite all the help received, I was in pain the following morning. Changing a patio into flower beds took grit and determination, and we were both sore and tired when the job was done.

I was thinking about this when the Israelites came to mind. God had promised them a new land that took forty years of wandering for them to see. There was still a lot of work to be done once they'd received the title to their property. I am sure they suffered a great deal of pain as they renovated their promised land. God had delivered the long awaited promise; now they needed to possess the land or make it their own. There were rocks in the form of unbelief to be removed; and underneath were the anthills that needed to be eradicated. Those pesky little creatures of fear and doubt wreak havoc in a healthy garden; they may even prevent healthy plants from reaching maturity.

Most of the rocks in my garden were lying on top of the soil; someone had placed them there. Now they were shifting and needed to be leveled; the only plant life that had ever been consistent was weeds because good growth requires nurturing and tenderness. The soil must be worked, and watched on a consistent and regular schedule. In the parable of the sower, the importance of soil preparation is emphasized. Tragic things happened on the unprepared soil. All the plants and seed in the world would not produce anything of quality in hard, rock-filled soil.

What an amazing result! The reward for aching sore knees and tired muscles is a bountiful crop. That was my goal when I looked at my yard, and that is my goal as I consider the garden of my life.

The gardener

". . . When I looked for good grapes, why did
it yield only bad. . . . I will take away its
hedge, and it will be destroyed; I will break
down its wall, and it will be trampled..."
(Isaiah 5: 4&5, NIV)

They were going to lose everything! Isaiah painted a bleak picture for the Israelites. God was unhappy with them because of their evil and unjust actions. Instead of producing wholesome fruit, the gardens had produced bitter fruit not fit for human consumption. They'd become selfish and did not act like God's people should.

The Israelites were caught in their sin! They'd done what they were told not to do, losing all godly perspective. Judgment was coming! What the gardeners had thought was success was no success at all!

We are frequently referred to as a garden planted by the Lord. This garden has a wall around it for protection. The marauders, thieves, and strong winds cannot enter. These walls are meant to aid us in producing superb fruit, but the garden still needs to be tended. The soil must be worked regularly so that weeds cannot take root. If nothing is done, then weeds can destroy whatever good has been started in our garden. There is no room for laziness in this garden; it requires hard work and long hours to ensure the right amounts of moisture, and nourishment are available.

Our soil must be turned up and worked through, keeping it soft. When the rain comes, we are better able to receive the watering of the Holy Spirit than if we'd simply waited for something to happen! Nutrition is ensured as we spend time in God's Word, searching for the vitamins and minerals our garden needs to sustain good growth.

We must strive to maintain a balance in our garden between the big, more rapid growth, and the slower, deeper growth that takes longer to bear fruit. All plants require room to grow, and we must be diligent to allow equal opportunities for development. God, himself, works in our lives. Sometimes it is through a divine move of His Holy Spirit while at other times people speak into our lives the words of life that we need to hear to continue to grow. God wants us to be balanced people, and have continued growth; and an abundant production of good fruit. Let's begin today to become good gardeners of our hearts.

Gardening

". . . He causes his sun to rise on the evil and
the good, and sends rain on the righteous
and the unrighteous."
(Matthew 5:45, NIV)

Gardening is a lot of work! In spring we wait for the ground to thaw and then dry out. This year, amid the torrential rains, we planted seed and an assortment of bedding out plants. Did we pray for rain? Perhaps we were too intense in our prayers. Now all we need is some warmer weather so that the ground will warm up and our plants will be able to grow and produce food for our tables and flowers to brighten our day.

I stripped sod this year in the hopes of having a flowerbed where there hadn't been one, and then I planted seed. Then the rain came, and I watched the ground with the expectation of seeing good plants emerge. After all the rain, the only plants to show up were......weeds! I eyed them carefully for a few days, wondering all the while if my flower plants would poke through the ground.

Eventually, I pulled the undesirables away from the good plants that were struggling for life. All this reminds me of what it is like as Christians.

Good seed has been planted in our lives. The rain of the Holy Spirit has come and watered the parched ground. We look for good fruit to emerge; but to our dismay, all we see are the undesirables, the weeds. Down on our knees we go, trying very hard to uproot the things that are threatening to choke out good fruit. It certainly would be easier to dig up the entire flower bed than to dig up the weeds and transplant the good stuff. Sometimes we need to let the weeds and the desirable plants grow until the good plants are able to withstand the stress of a changing environment. In the same way God allows the undesirable things in our lives to grow until we have gained sufficient strength from Him to withstand the change.

Just like gardening is a lot of work, so is the work involved as we set our goal on becoming more like Christ. The weeds requiring demolition will not let go without a struggle, but our lives will become richer and more productive if we remain persistent in rooting out the undesirable elements in our lives.

M. JOYCE HALVORSON

The grapevine

"I am the true vine, and my Father is the
gardener. He cuts off every branch in me
that bears no fruit, while every branch that
does bear fruit he prunes so that it will be
even more fruitful. . . No branch can bear
fruit by itself; it must remain in the vine. . .
. I am the vine; you are the branches."
(John 15: 1-2, 4-5, NIV)

I've never seen grapevines or vineyards. But I've been told that they are a lot of hard work. The nice neat rows of grapes are the result of countless hours and days of painstaking labor and patience. The grapevine's natural tendency is towards wild and ragged growth. They will grow just about anywhere and will wrap their branches around the nearest tree. There is life in the undisciplined, free wheeling branches. There is even some fruit. Yet, this fruit is often very small and quite bitter. Experts tell us that the branches must be trimmed and pruned on a regular basis so that the life giving energy found within the branches is sent to those areas that can produce the best fruit.

All this reminds me of the way it is with us as Christians. Many times we wonder at the problems we encounter and we wonder why we are encountering difficulty in what we see as a ministry. It could be that God is allowing this difficulty in an effort to prune some of our growth. The life in the superfluous branches has been taking vitality away from the fruit. We have become so busy with activity that our life has drained away necessary energy and nutrition from more important areas in our lives. We are not as effective as we could be in God's kingdom.

Father, please come and take up residence in our vineyards. We give you permission to cut back the activities in our lives so that we can divert our energy into more meaningful endeavors. When things go wrong, Father, remind us of the pruning taking place in our lives. We want to produce the biggest and the best fruit, not puny, and inferior, sour grapes. As you put your healing salve on the open cuts, heal us and bring closure to those areas that are no longer as meaningful as they once were. We want to remain in Jesus, the true vine and source of life.

Seeds

"... unless a kernel of wheat falls to the ground and dies, it remains only a single seed. But if it dies, it produces many seeds."
(John 12:24, NIV)

My neighbor gave me a bag full of carrots fresh from her garden. They came complete with the tops, roots, and mud still attached. I cleaned them up and cut the tops and roots off, leaving a small bowl full of the delectable and crunchy orange vegetable. I thought about their origin as I cleaned them. The tiny seeds seemed lifeless. What good could come from what appeared to be almost nothing? The seeds were dropped into the soil, covered, watered, and left to grow. They would produce their fruit in good time. Had my neighbor held the packet of seeds in her hand, refusing to allow the seeds to die, they would not reproduce.

The same is true of our lives as Christians. Good seed (God's Word) is planted in us, producing early signs of new life. We are ecstatic! Yet, what we initially saw as a sign of new growth must first die. We need to surrender, and let our dreams die before God can resurrect them and bring new life into them. Those dreams are some of the seed that God has planted in our own lives. Giving them back to God has the appearance of burying them, or of allowing them to die. But it is only once we have surrendered our rights to those dreams that God can use them. It is He that gave them to us. What he expects from us is trust in His unfailing love and faithfulness. He will not abandon us. He will complete the work that He has begun in us. But it all begins with a seed, a tiny glimmer of something we can do for God. After surrendering this hope we can fully expect fruit to come in due time. Just like the carrots took time to appear, so we must be patient and allow God to cause new growth to appear in our lives.

Father, I give you my dreams, my hopes, and my desires. They are yours. You placed those dreams within me, and now, I give them back to you. Cause resurrected life to blossom within me, producing an abundant harvest of luscious fruit.

Flowers? or Weeds?

"... a man who sowed good seed in his field.
... his enemy came and sowed weeds..
. when the wheat sprouted and formed
heads, then the weeds also appeared....
while you are pulling the weeds, you may
root up the wheat with them. Let both
grow together until the harvest. At that
time ... collect the weeds ... to be burned,
then gather the wheat and bring it."
(Matthew 13:24-30, NIV)

I was weeding my flower bed the other day. Some weeds were by themselves and were easy to pull out of the moist earth, while other weeds were so close to the good plant that if I'd pulled the weed, I would have destroyed the plant I wanted to keep.

We cannot eradicate all sin as long as we are in this world. In our zeal to stand for what is right we must be careful to not damage the tender plants struggling for survival. They are tender fragile shoots of righteousness that are just beginning to show signs of life. Their environment must be carefully nurtured, ensuring the right amount of nutrients and water. We do not expect a new shoot to withstand extreme weather conditions; neither should we expect those who are only beginning to show spiritual growth to withstand pressure and upheaval around them.

What is right before God and what is not right receive equal amounts of rain as the Holy Spirit rains down on us. The good plants will receive vital nourishment, and the ground it will become saturated with His presence. It is in such an atmosphere that the weeds in our lives can be more readily removed. The roots of weeds are often deeply imbedded and are more easily removed with a good soaking. They will lose their ability to remain embedded once the earth is softened. God is faithful and He will begin the tug, removing unwanted weeds in our lives.

What stage of growth are we entering? Are we fragile shoots requiring tender care, or are we in the mature, ready-to-harvest, stage? We must put away the umbrellas and allow the Holy Spirit to rain upon us, bringing us the required nourishment. The weeds in our lives will be dealt with as we allow Him to have complete control in our lives.

Transplanting

".. They will be called oaks of righteousness,
a planting of the Lord ..."
(Isaiah 61:3, NIV)

A few weeks ago I took a quick trip to a greenhouse near where I live. I wanted perennials – plants that come up every year. You see, I am tired of buying "throwaway" plants. I did the same last year, and the flower bed didn't look very good. This year the difference is amazing! My one flowerbed is now crowded with new growth. I've even been able to give away some of the produce! This year, my new plants were taken out of their temporary homes and transplanted into their new home in another of my flower beds. They looked sad at first, and now with all the rain we've had, they've perked up and are doing ok. The plants look lonely right now and the flower bed looks naked. But I am anticipating a wonderful return next year.

All this kind of reminds me of our walk with God. Seeds are planted by the Holy Spirit in what appears to be a small confined space in our hearts. They appear to be dead, worthless bits of information. These seemingly worthless bits of information are then watered by the Holy Spirit, and the ground is warmed by the Son's warm rays. For a while, it appears that nothing is going to grow. Suddenly, a tiny, fragile shoot appears, then another; soon the ground is filled with plants growing and reaching upward. For a while, all appears to be wonderful! God is doing great things in the flowerbed; the plants are producing amazing fruit. Then the time comes that the healthy fruit appears to be ill and loses its luster. Instead of medicating it with more vitamins and tender loving care, the mature plant is taken out of its original setting and placed in a new space. It has been transplanted.

It looks lonely. There are no other similar plants around providing it with warmth and protection. It is truly alone, and cannot understand. Eventually, new and stronger root systems are established and this plant once again flourishes, surrounded by new friends in the Plant Kingdom. This lonely plant that once felt so isolated did not die, but reproduced itself all around it. It is no longer lonely but sees life full of promise and revels in the place where it has been transplanted.

M. JOYCE HALVORSON

Holy spirit moments

"Those who live according to the sinful nature have their minds set on what that nature desires; but those who live in accordance with the Spirit have their minds set on what the Spirit desires. The mind controlled by the Spirit is life and peace......... You .... are controlled not by the sinful nature but by the Spirit of God."
(Romans 8:5-9, NIV)

A few weeks ago I asked for some time off: I only needed the morning, but asked for the entire day – just in case. One of my appointments was moved to the afternoon the morning of the original appointment. On a more serious note, Wilf, a friend, was at the church a while ago for a meeting that didn't happen. He thought he'd check the sump pump while he was waiting for the others to show up. To his dismay the pump had quit working, and the water was half an inch from seeping into the basement. The meeting never took place, but because he was at the church, we were spared another flooded basement!

The Holy Spirit prompted me to ask for the entire day off, because He knew I would need it. Furthermore, it was the Holy Spirit that orchestrated the meeting that never happened; Wilf was at the church and checked on a vital piece of equipment at a critical time. There was no coincidence about it; it's called living and walking in the Spirit. This elusive concept of walking in the Spirit is a very practical thing, one we cannot live without. It is for every believer.

When we belong to Christ, we are set to please God. This isn't always something that we make a conscious decision to do – we just do it. It's an automatic leading of the Holy Spirit. Living in the Spirit does not mean we are walking around like people from another planet; we function as normal human beings with the added advantage of the Holy Spirit at work in our lives, leading and directing us. It's our inheritance from Jesus, and it is a continual thing, and not something we are aware of occurring. The above passage is an amazing passage of scripture. It settles who we are in Christ. We are Christ's; therefore, we are lead by the Spirit and we have more Holy Spirit moments than we realize. It's exciting!

In hot pursuit!

"You will seek me and find me when you
seek me with all your heart."
(Jeremiah 29:13, NIV)

I like watching detective shows. One such TV show was particularly intriguing! The perpetrator of the crime deliberately left clues as to his identity. He would leave notes and poetry each with a clue as to the whereabouts of the victim and to his own identity. Tension mounted as the valiant detectives worked around the clock trying hard to solve the puzzle before the certain death of the victim. They missed the deadlines and eventually found the victim – too late! Of course the good guys always win, but not until they'd grilled the perpetrator who'd let himself be caught. He'd just wanted attention; he'd wanted to be notorious so that his books would be published. The case was successfully solved because of the diligence and perseverance of the people involved.

The above scripture reminds us of quite another search. The Israelites had experienced persecution and famine. Then Jeremiah gives them the message that after seventy years God will bring them deliverance on one condition: If they would seek God with all their hearts. God did not want part time people. He wanted to be passionately pursued. He wanted a people that would drop everything else in their pursuit of Him. The message hasn't changed since Jeremiah first delivered it. God wants to be pursued. He's even left clues as to his whereabouts: extraordinary worship services, sinners repenting without a formal invitation to do so, supernatural manifestations of his presence. The list could go on and on. God wants to be pursued, but far more importantly, He wants to be caught. He wants us to become so desperate for His presence that we will not be satisfied with just a glimpse of glory or a taste of His presence.

What God wants is for His people to really know Him, and to delight spending time in His presence. He wants fellowship with us. You know the sort of thing where we just sit and talk about anything and everything. Words don't seem to matter much because He understands what we are trying to say. He wants to hang out with us and wants us to do the same with Him. He will never disappoint us. He is waiting with open arms. Are you in pursuit?

Maps

Maps are great inventions – a person just needs to be able to read one. To the uninitiated, they resemble some toddlers' writing efforts. They are important tools, however, in determining how to get from one place to another, particularly if you've never been there before. At times I am sure I would continually drive around in circles without a map on the seat beside me.

Even when we know how to read a map, we must be willing to change our location. All the maps in the world would not have helped me if I had not been willing to leave Airdrie. When on vacation in Ontario, I would never have found my way from Walkerton to Niagara Falls, and subsequently to Ottawa had I refused to leave Walkerton.

The Bible is like a map, with added instructions in it. We are told how to live in our relationships, and are given directions on how to find peace, love, joy, and many other things. The problem is that many people have never read it. They rely solely on what their friends and family tell them. Then they say that it is too hard to understand, and far too complicated. There are several contemporary translations available that makes it much easier to read. It's like reading a road map. The more a person reads it, the easier it becomes to understand what we are reading.

Another difficulty encountered is that we might read the Bible, but we refuse to follow its guidelines. I'll do it my way is our anthem as we continue to berate what we consider outdated. The Bible, our map for living, is only as effective as we allow it to be. We must put into practice what we have read on its pages.

Maps can be fascinating to read, and the Bible, a map or guideline for living, can be even more fascinating as we discover excitement and adventure on its pages. Life becomes a new adventure every day, and the rest we need so badly becomes ours as we choose to change our way of living and follow the greatest map of all times.

Dirt diggin'

"Although the Lord gives you the bread of
adversity and the water of affliction, your
teachers will be hidden no more; with your
own eyes you will see them. Whether you
turn to the right or to the left, your ears
will hear a voice behind you, saying, 'This is
the way; walk in it.'"
(Isaiah 30:20-21, NIV)

With all the road construction going on around my home city of
Airdrie, I got to thinking about all the similarities between that
and our walk with the Lord.

A new way - Traffic continued while a new route was put
in place for the north and south off ramps. A lot of dirt was
moved around until just the right route was in place. Our lives
are seemingly torn up as God prepares a new way for us to walk.
Discomfort and pain are experienced as our lives are rearranged
to accommodate change.

Durability - The first heavy rain would make a dirt track impassable, so the surface was paved for durability. Before the layer of asphalt was laid, heavy equipment ran over the dirt track, developing a solid base. Discomfort and pain are experienced as pressure and the gentle rain of the Holy Spirit are applied so that our lives become an inviting pathway to God. If we had no problems or difficulties, we would remain soft, and the first bout of opposition would cause us to become a soupy mess, hence the benefits of trials.

New signs – Signs are prepared in advance of the new off ramp opening. We were aware of the direction we'd be taking as we left the highway.

Sometimes, in our haste to do "great things for God", we become confused when our way is blocked. It could be that we've missed the signs along the way.

The old way becomes extinct – The old way is now blocked to traffic. No one is allowed there, and the road is torn up. We must be careful to hear what the Holy Spirit is saying to us. Our past is our past, and cannot be entirely relied upon. The old way is gone forever, with the way being torn up to make way for new construction.

> "... do not dwell on the past. See, I am doing a new thing! I am making a way in the desert and streams in the wasteland"
>
> (Isaiah 43:18-19, NIV)

M. JOYCE HALVORSON

Potholes

*". . In the desert prepare the way for the
Lord; make straight in the wilderness a
highway for our God. Every valley shall be
raised up, every mountain and hill made
low; the rough ground shall become level,
the rugged places a plain. And the glory of
the Lord will be revealed, and all mankind
together will see it. For the mouth of the
Lord has spoken."*
(Isaiah 40: 3 & 4, NIV)

'Tis the season for potholes. It isn't as bad this year as in other years. But there they are - tire wreckers and rim benders! My fire-fly had aluminium rims. They were much softer (unfortunately) than other types. On the way to the church I couldn't miss one pothole for hitting a worse one. Twice that resulted in expensive repairs on the rims. Sometimes, more serious damage can result to a vehicle. Accidents happen as drivers over compensate for a sudden jolt. Potholes are generally unavoidable. Usually the pothole patrol drives around filling in these holes in the road. Temporary fixes, the roadway eventually becomes pitted and the entire roadway is dug up and replaced. All this annual potholing makes it difficult to get to where a person wants to go.

We are like those potholes. Instead of preparing the way, making it easy, for the Lord to come and for people to come to Him, we have prepared obstacles. Some, climbing out of the valley of despair, have not found a helping hand. Instead, Mount Everest looms ahead. I am not suggesting that we must water down our standards. What I am saying is that let's uncomplicate the process. Salvation, deliverance for body, soul and spirit, is free. There is nothing anyone can do to earn it. Let's remove the conditions we've made for acceptance and begin loving people where they are. Let's show them the way to the cross. Let's remove all the conditions for acceptance into the kingdom of God. Instead of causing a seeker to stumble, let's fill in the holes.

Salvation will come to our community as we begin to remove the potholes and mountains. The gravel of pride will disappear as we begin to make the way easier to find for those around us.

Angels unaware

"For he will command his angels concerning you to guard you in all your ways; they will lift you up in their hands, so that you will not strike your foot against a stone."
(Psalm 91:11, NIV)

I was driving home from work around 11:15 pm. It was dark, and very foggy. I am a creature of habit and usually take the same way home; but that evening I had decided to take a different way to Deerfoot Trail. By the time I'd reached 64 Avenue, the traffic had slowed considerably and I found myself behind a transport truck. I said, "Thank you, Jesus." and proceeded to follow it north. With its bright red marker lights piercing the fog between us, I felt safe. About half way home we caught up to another transport truck. The first one changed lanes and sped off into the foggy night. I followed the second truck until I reached the turnoff to Airdrie, at which point that truck also picked up speed. I found it quite interesting that I would find two vehicles on my way home because those were the type that I knew could lead the way when I was floundering.

Since that time I've wondered whether those truckers were aware that they'd given me such a blessing. It's really hard to say. Were they angels?

> "The king's heart is in the hand of the Lord; he directs it like a watercourse wherever he pleases."
>
> (Proverbs 21:1, NIV)

My paraphrase would read: the truckers' hearts are in the hands of the Lord; he directs them like a watercourse wherever he pleases [if Joyce needs a guiding light, then he can direct a trucker or two to provide just that.] They probably weren't angels, but they were directed by God.

God does provide for us in many small ways. I wonder how long our list would be if, just for a week, we gave God the credit (or glory) for all the little things in our lives that work out just right. It's easy to take all these little things for granted. True thankfulness does not only include the really big stuff; it begins with the small, seemingly insignificant incidents in our lives.

When I gave thanks for the "guiding lights" in my life that night, I felt like a spoiled King's kid! He loves to spoil me. At least that's my opinion. Have a great day with the Lord.

Headlights

"Your word is a lamp to my feet and a light
for my path."
(Psalm 119:105, NIV)

The drive in to the city for work can be quite interesting. It had snowed during the night and it was foggy in patches. I wasn't even tempted to exceed the speed limit. The headlights on my car provided sufficient light for the immediate vicinity. The windshield washers were in frequent use, and still my vision was obscured. All this brought back memories of driving in "white out" conditions. In these situations my headlights aren't very effective in lighting my way; they can only light my immediate vicinity.

God's Word is so much like my headlights; it lights the immediate vicinity. The promises and instructions contained within its pages provide answers for our immediate problems and concerns. It is interesting to note that the word, lamp, in the above verse refers to a candle which is something that we are responsible to maintain. We must make the effort to get into God's Word and find the answers.

It is our responsibility to study the Bible and apply it to our lives. Just like a candle that can be blown out, so we must be careful to constantly fan the flame that is ignited in our hearts as we allow Scripture to become our manna, our daily bread. There are many different translations of the Bible on the market; find one that is easy to read and understand and make it your source of spiritual food.

The headlights on my car need perfect conditions to light the way very much beyond the immediate. They are ineffective at shining over a rise in the road or around a corner. God's Word goes beyond the immediate and gives us light for the future. It illuminates our entire lives and is not limited by our understanding. It is the sun shining brightly and causes our lives to become alive and buoyant with happiness and joy.

The truth remains. What begins with a seemingly small and insignificant movement on our part in reading the Bible becomes the spark that has changed lives for generations and will set our lives ablaze with light. We will never be the same again. We will be changed forever, and it all begins with two four letter words – READ the WORD!

Persistence

"Brothers, I do not consider myself yet to have taken hold of it. But one thing I do: forgetting what is behind and straining toward what is ahead, I press on toward the goal to win the prize for which God has called me heavenward in Christ Jesus."
(Philippians 3: 13 &14, NIV)

I do a lot of quilting. Right now I am working on a quilt that is causing me some grief. Things aren't going as well as I had hoped they would, and I've had to back track, remove stitching, and cut some new pieces. I haven't given up, and eventually, those nail-biting, hair – graying pieces of fabric will be part of a wonderful creation. There is an awesome picture or a completed quilt in my mind, and that is what I am working towards.

I have virtually forgotten the pieces of the quilt that were trashed, and made some new ones. Was it easy to do? No! It was aggravating to have to repeat myself, but I did it anyway. I had to admit I'd erred. But I didn't get stuck in the erring. I corrected what I could and carried on. Just like quilting takes perseverance and patience, so growing in God takes persistence. We are responsible to confess the sin in our lives, and discard or repent from them. It may seem as though we are going backwards, but it's only temporary. Because God will create a new piece which is much more beneficial to the plan he has for us. Speed is not important. What matters is that we keep walking the path laid out for us, and that we finish the race.

It would have been rather silly of me to selfishly hang on to the faulty quilt pieces. It would have destroyed the finished quilt. In the same way we must let go of the things that God points out to us. He wants to complete us so that we can be the very best possible. Let's allow Him to do what he wants in our lives. As we surrender the torn pieces of our lives He will replace them with something brand new. Let's trust God to finish the work He has begun in us. Let's keep our eyes on the goal.

Praise reports

I work with an impressive assortment of people and personalities. We talk about all kinds of things as we go about our business of health care. Sometimes their opinions are of absolutely no value; while at other times what they have to say is of infinite value. I have learned profound principles from Christians and non-Christians alike. It is a privilege to work in such an environment.

All too frequently, we reject what our non-Christian friends have to say – simply because they are not Christians. What good can their advice be if they are not walking with God? In this verse, Paul is saying that we should think about anything that is worth while remembering. Is it important to remember sordid details of a party? Not in my books! But I love to hear of a son or daughter's success at school or in the workplace. Then there was the rise to fame in the popular show, Canadian Idol, of the nephew of a co-worker – Billy Klippert. It was exciting because I know his aunt who was justifiably proud of her family member. Is he a Christian? I doubt it. But is his news praiseworthy? I think so.

What is praiseworthy? It could be defined as anything positive, constructive, or upbeat that is worth while repeating. Personally, I am thankful for my good health and my friends. God has been good to me. Like a chorus I sang as a youngster: God is so good, God is so good, God is so good, He's so good to me.

In Philippians we are instructed to meditate on, or give a home to, those things that are praiseworthy. It's exciting to hear of a family member succeeding. It is equally as exciting to hear of how God answered prayer, healing someone or a relationship. I love to hear of God's provision and can provide many such stories from my personal experience. All these things are praiseworthy. They do not bring anyone or anything down. They don't throw mud or blacken a name. Paul encourages us to think about, or meditate on, or ruminate on, these things. Then a few sentences later, he tells us that if we do these things, we will have God's peace. Try it today – it's worth the effort.

Precious memories

"I have been reminded of your sincere faith,
which first lived in your grandmother
Lois and in your mother Eunice and, I am
persuaded, now lives in you also."
(2 Timothy 1: 5, NIV)

I love listening to older people recount the early days of their Christian experience. I also love listening to anyone relating an experience of God meeting their needs after they'd been obedient to God's Word. In the days when books and recordings were not in existence, this was how memories and traditions were passed down to the next generation. People recounted, or told, what had transpired in their lives.

Paul wrote about a similar situation in 2 Timothy when he says he was reminded. Timothy had an incredible heritage. Two generations before him had served God. It was no doubt these two generations that had passed on to him all the good things God had done. His generation was the third.

While not all of us can lay claim to such a rich heritage, some can. Personally, I cannot tire of hearing the "old testimonies". They amaze me as much today as when I first heard them. It should be that way for all of us. We love to hear that God is doing a new thing, but what we fail to realize is that most often He is building upon the foundations laid for us by our ancestors in the faith.

Yes, God is doing a new thing. But it is the faith of those who've gone before us, and the testimonies of God's goodness towards us that inspire and bolster our own faith. First generation Christians need not be ashamed, but ought to hold their heads high and proclaim what God has done, and is doing, in their lives.

The early church met frequently and shared their experiences, and so must we. Whenever we are together, let's share what God has done in our lives. Let's not assume people already know, and let's not allow the devil to talk us into thinking that our testimonies are too small and insignificant.

Memories, old and new alike, are precious. When all is quiet and darkness prevails, memories flood our minds and bring comfort. Precious memories – very old or most recent—bolster our faith and lift sagging spirits. Let's begin today to build our storehouse of precious memories. Let's share what God has done!

What we remember

> *"And these words, which I command you today shall be in your heart; you shall teach them diligently to your children, and shall talk of them when you sit in your house, and when you walk by the way, and when you lie down, and when you rise up."*
> *(Deuteronomy 6:6&7, NKJV)*

It was so familiar! I looked at the verse I was to memorize as part of a Bible Study and began to sing it! My late teen years and into my early twenties were spent singing scripture. We were at the tail end of what we called the "Jesus Movement" and those involved loved to sing scripture. That was a lot of years ago and I can still recall those scripture songs.

The Israelites had a problem. They had no books with which to teach their children God's laws, and they had no way of recording their history so that their descendants would remember what they'd been told and experienced. God instructed Moses to tell the Children of Israel to be careful to teach their offspring.

Some of their teaching must have taken the form of music because music is so much more palatable than just saying something repeatedly. First they had to know what it was they were teaching; then they were to teach their own families. The next thing I noticed was that it was to be a continual instruction; daily conversation, showing the children the way to live and conduct their lives. There didn't seem to be very much preaching, just instruction or teaching children by example.

In much the same way we are to daily instruct those who are following us, children, new Christians alike. Our daily conversation and the way in which we conduct our lives go a long way in spreading the Good News. Sometimes we may even draw comparisons between the natural world and that which we do not see – the spirit world. It is these daily times that seem so small and insignificant that have a great impact on people. Years later, these same people will recall just such moment with us, one we've long forgotten.

It's an exciting and challenging responsibility that has been given to us by God. We are to teach continually, when we are relaxing and when we are working. When we are sure of whom we are, it takes such little effort to teach others. Are you up to the challenge?

M. JOYCE HALVORSON

Puzzling people

"You did not choose me, but I chose you to
go and bear fruit – fruit that will last."
(John 15:16a, NIV)

My father and I are puzzling people. We love to break open a new puzzle box and sort through the pieces. Before we get very far, we prop the picture on the top of the box where we can see it. Then we usually put the outside pieces, or frame, together and finally begin everything else. Dad loves to do the sky and I generally look for the more colorful and easier pieces. Sometimes we have been forced to undo some of our hard work. What we thought belonged in a particular corner doesn't belong there at all. Eventually the picture becomes clear and we admire our handiwork.

Life tends to be that way as well. We are born with the outside edge, or framework. As we grow and mature the borders of our lives become more pronounced. Gradually the rest of it is filled in, one piece at a time, until the masterpiece is finished. What began at birth continues throughout our lives.

Our parameters are clearly stated in scripture. We were created to honor and serve God. Our entire lives are to be lives of worship—an offering to God. Beyond the parameters that everyone has, the pictures rapidly change. We are unique, and are made for a very specific purpose.

We did not choose our framework; God did. He handpicked each of the pieces that would make the masterpiece uniquely ours. Just when we think our masterpiece is coming together wonderfully well, we find ourselves being torn apart; the beauty no longer there. Over time we find transformation in an area of our lives that was incomplete, and more pieces are added. This process takes place repeatedly, and each phase is just a little more beautiful than the one previously.

There will be hills, valleys and mountain tops in our picture. We will navigate quiet streams and raging rivers. There will be green grass where we will find peace and rest; and there will be deserts we must traverse. We will not always understand why we travel where we do. Just remember that Jesus knows our weaknesses and our strengths. He is the only one who can see the outcome because he holds the final picture in his hands.

M. JOYCE HALVORSON

The rat race

"All men will know you are my disciples if
you love one another."
(John 13:35, NIV)

We all know people who are extremely busy with their careers. They seldom have time for a relaxing evening with family or friends. The eight hour work day is foreign to them and so is the 5 day work week. Their hours look more like 16 or 18 hours each day and sometimes 7 days a week. The parties they attend are more a business meeting than a social event. All this, they say, is so that their families can have more things or go more places. We call them workaholics.

Then there are people who, having shunned the rat race of this world, involve themselves in church activities and the work of the ministry. They have little time for their families, claiming the cause of Christ is far more important than spending time at home or going to games with their children. They spend hours in Bible Studies, and in preparing for a Sunday School lesson. No time for Mark or Suzy. We call them committed.

Both groups of people are caught! They have become part of the rat race. The secular rat race is certainly much more easily defined. Yet, the Christian rat race is equally as damaging to the strength of our families. I am not saying that we should all become couch potatoes and depend upon the government for support. Neither am I saying that we do not need Sunday School teachers or Worship leaders or Bible Study leaders. We need them all. But we must also remember the order our priorities should take.

We see the needs around us and long to do something about them. Questions we should ask before beginning a new project or ministry are: How will this impact my family? Will I still have time to spend with each person? Have I given opportunity for each family member to voice their opinions? Have I prayed about it? As Christians we must set the example for our family members and neighbours in the way we care for each other. We cannot neglect our own homes and expect to see God move in our churches and communities.

Let's strive to find the correct balance for our lives. The people we rub shoulders with will see our love for our family and for others. Then they will know whose we are.

Run to daddy

"I will say of the Lord, 'He is my refuge and my fortress, my God, in whom I trust.'"
(Psalm 91:2, NIV)

A little girl is running around in the open field. Her arms are stretched out wide as she joyfully experiences the breezes ruffling her hair. She laughs as she watches the birds building nest and gophers poking their head out of their holes. The sky is a brilliant blue with only a few clouds far away on the horizon. Gradually the clouds become larger and begin drifting towards the open field. The closer they are to the area where the young child is playing, the darker they become. It is obvious to anyone that a storm is imminent. Soon, the little girl notices the dark clouds and becomes frightened. There is danger in the clouds and she starts running. Where is she running to? As we watch the scene changing, some arms, her daddy's, appear before her. They are held wide open, waiting for the moment that she is close enough to be picked up. There is safety and comfort in those arms. Nothing can harm the child as long as she is in those arms.

We are like that little girl. Life is great and we are busy. There are no immediate dangers to threaten our happiness, and we breathe in deeply as we live our lives. However, we fail to notice the clouds forming because we have become accustomed to seeing those big, white, fluffy things overhead. They have changed, and now are full of danger. It could be false guilt or the incriminations of the enemy. Either way, we are now in imminent danger. Should we continue the way we are? Do we run and, if so, where? God is waiting for us with open arms. He is waiting for us to run to him so He can pick us up. There is safety and security in those arms.

Whenever we choose to run with abandon straight into the waiting arms of God, we have chosen the only sure place of safety. It will never change, and will always be there for us. The choice is ours. We can try to do things our way and in our own strength, or we can run into the waiting arms of our Heavenly Father where there is peace and safety.

M. JOYCE HALVORSON

Still waters run deep

". . . he leads me beside quiet waters, he
restores my soul."
(Psalm 23:2, NIV)

My husband and his siblings were raised on a farm without running water. I remember being told that we had to let the freshly pumped water sit in the pail for awhile before it was drinkable. The water became warm as it sat still. The strategy was to let all the sand and other impurities sink to the bottom; then the water was good to drink. The good clear drinking water was worth the wait. The same is true of almost any body of water; the sediment settles to the bottom. Rushing rivers tend to carry the garbage along as it roars through its channels, and only the foolhardy would dare swimming in it. Quiet waters attract swimmers and sunbathers. There is something calming about relaxing along its banks.

God was intending for us to relax and become refreshed. Our

spirits and our souls are replenished as we sit and rest beside the quiet waters God provides. There is no rushing around and no anxious thoughts, neither is there very much activity or sound. It is quiet – it would appear that God is not nearby. Yet, He is because it is He that has provided the slowed pace. He calls us today to come to the waters and stay by his side. He knows we are thirsty and He won't deny us what we need.

Isn't it interesting that our souls are restored in the quietness, and not in the activity? We are led into inactivity so that we can rest beside the water that life-giving force. We can drink whenever we are thirsty, and then rest again. This scene is repeated until we are completely refreshed and strengthened. There is no worry about the water running out because God's supply is endless. There is no hurry; this process cannot be rushed by our long list of things to do. We must rest and wait for our souls to be renewed.

The grass beside the quiet waters is green, lush, and inviting. It is cool and yet we are warmed by the sun. We have everything we need, and yet we have nothing, because nothing but ourselves is required. He leads us into restoration. He leads us because He cares for us.

M. JOYCE HALVORSON

Togethering

"Take your turn, with no one person taking over. That way each one gets a chance to say something special from God, and you all learn from each other."
(Corinthians 14:30-31, The Message)

Friends of all ages travel together, sharing a common interest in their destination, and taking pleasure in each other's company. I traveled to Ontario a few years ago in solitary pursuit of friends who'd moved "down east". I saw much of what I'd previously only read or heard about. Upon arrival in Brighton, I learned that I was a mere 3½-hour drive away from our nation's capital. My friend and I drove there together; that day trip is still in my bank of favorite memories. We laughed together and shared the "work of driving".

As Christians we can get along just fine, at least for a while, all on our own. We can read the Bible, pray, and learn to hear God speak to us. Then a crisis arrives in our lives, and we discover that our own wisdom and strength are not enough to see us through the tough time. We become frustrated people, angry that no one has come to our aid, when in fact we have not made an attempt at becoming part of a community or small group. In these settings we learn to depend on each other and enjoy the give and take of relationship. Then when a problem arises, we have someone to turn to. At times it may only be a listening ear or a soft shoulder to lean on. On other occasions, we may need much more help, but we will already have formed our base for support.

It's great being a part of a small group of Christians. We laugh and play together; we also cry together and share our sorrows and problems. We've heard a lot about the importance of small groups, yet so many of us still tend to go our own way. It's so much more enjoyable when joys and sorrows alike are shared. It's in togethering that bonds are formed and spiritual growth becomes the norm. We learn accountability with our family of close friends, and we are not alone anymore.

M. JOYCE HALVORSON

Walls

"My sheep listen to my voice; I know them,
and they follow me."
(John 10:27, NIV)

I love the story of Nehemiah. He gave up a life of luxury in the King's palace to lead his people in rebuilding the walls around Jerusalem. He persevered through criticism, false accusation, discouragement, attacks, and on and on. He stuck it out. That wall was crucial in protecting the residents from constant invasion and marauding rebels. They'd previously rebuilt the temple. Yet, this wall had to be built for protection. It was no easy task and certainly no job for a morning of cleaning and renovations. It took a long time.

Then I started thinking about all the walls we've built around ourselves. Most of them must be torn down because they prevent us from being who we were meant to be and keep us from living life fully. A good wall, the kind God wants us to build, will not prevent us from experiencing life, but will protect us from Satan's attack on our lives. What is the wall made of, and how is it built?

Each relationship we form with someone is a brick in that wall. When we need some honest advice, there is someone to turn to. When we are hurting, there is someone to comfort us. When we need help, that help is available to us. God designed us with the need for relationships with others. We cannot live our lives independent of relationships. We tend to withdraw when we've been hurt. Yet, it is when we choose to isolate ourselves and maintain independence exclusive of anyone else that we fall, and fail miserably. It is in this place that Satan can begin to destroy who we are.

Daily Bible reading and prayer is another brick we place in our walls. It is in the study of God's Word and in fellowship with Him that we learn to hear his voice. This, too, takes time. As we learn to recognize His voice, we will not be easily swayed by life's circumstances, and Satan will not be able to rob us of what is rightfully ours.

> *"Your enemy the devil prowls around like a roaring lion looking for someone to devour."*
>
> (1 Peter 5:8, NIV)

Let's begin today to tear down the walls preventing God's blessing from reaching us and begin to build, brick by brick, those walls that will protect us from the enemy of our souls.

Walls - More of them!

"Where no counsel is, the people fall: but in the multitude of counsellors there is safety."
(Proverbs 11:14, KJV)

Nehemiah's wall was an incredible work of art, a testimony to the goodness of God. It was a wall ordained by God. It protected those within from attack of the enemy. Just like that wall in Nehemiah's day, we need walls around us today. There are walls around many of us that must be torn down because they are self make walls of stone. We've allowed the hurts and bitterness of life experiences to form a hard shell around us. These are the wrong walls and these are the walls that must come down. The wall that I am talking about is the kind that is built a little at a time, but it is necessary.

Some of the bricks in the wall are the relationships we form with others. We cannot be independent of our friends and family. We need each other. Daily Bible reading and prayer are additional bricks in our wall. These bricks prevent Satan from attacking with only partially accurate scripture while wholesome relationships form the network we need.

Honesty before God and with our friends is another key brick in our wall. We must be honest about how we are feeling and thinking. We push our emotions down when we deny we have been hurt. Eventually, our hurt and anger will erupt, probably inappropriately, wounding others. We can deal with our frustrations when we are honest. There will be nothing to erupt later. A counsellor commented that you have to be close to someone to shake your fist in their face. I was so angry at God that I had a vivid picture of doing just that. During this time in my life, I was assured by God that He loved me just the way I was and He understood. My relationship with Him would not have deepened had I not acknowledged my anger.

In being honest we also become vulnerable. It becomes very easy for us to be hurt. But because we are sensitive to our own wounds, we have become sensitive to others as well, thus making us stronger than before. The victory is ours as we unite together.

These bricks: honesty, vulnerability, relationships and Bible reading and prayer, are key bricks in our wall. They are part of our defence against the attacks of the wicked one.

DARE TO BE DIFFERENT

M. JOYCE HALVORSON

Comforters

"And I will pray the Father, and he shall give you another Comforter, that he may abide with you for ever;"
(John 14:16 KJV)

When I was a little girl, we had some smaller blankets that were used as an extra layer of warmth. Most often they were light quilts, and were never meant as a primary source of warmth. They were extra, and they were called comforters. Both my sons have some of these smaller quilts which were made for them by their grandmothers and great grandmother. In our household we had a blanket that I called the "get well quick" blanket. It was used only when either boy was sick and was lying on the couch. Eventually, it wore out and now it is no longer around. This was also another version of a quilt or comforter because it brought comfort when wrapped tightly around a person.

The Bible talks about another kind of comforter, the Holy Spirit. He was initially sent to Jesus' disciples because they were losing their leader, hence the term "comforter". They would feel lost and dejected because someone whom they loved had left them. Enter the Holy Spirit. He is much more than one person; He can be everywhere at the same time. Yet, the Holy Spirit brings comfort to the individual, to the person who has suffered a tragic loss.

Whenever I feel the need of comfort I tend to curl up on my loveseat, pulling a throw blanket (new word for comforter) around me. After a nap I feel much better. In much the same way the Holy Spirit comes around us and surrounds us, individually, bringing comfort and solace when we are in need of it. He lovingly pulls us into his arms and holds us close. All we are required to do is to accept his embrace. He gently rocks us and whispers words of love and comfort in our hearts. We must simply let go and allow ourselves to sink into the warmth and softness of his touch. The only place we can fall is into our Comforter. We must allow ourselves the luxury of accepting the gift of our Comforter. Unlike the small quilts with which we wrap ourselves, the Holy Spirit is big enough to surround each of us individually with plenty of room for one more.

Let's begin today to fall -- into the waiting warmth of our Comforter.

Exercise

"For this reason I remind you to fan into flame the gift of God, which is in you..."
(2 Timothy 1:6, NIV)

At the start of any season, sports enthusiasts get all excited about losing themselves in their favorite activity. Most of us seldom take the time to warm up our muscles before beginning said activity. There is little or no preparation before beginning; as a result we feel battered and bruised afterwards. Whenever we do any form of activity that we are not accustomed to, we use muscles that are dormant. They are not used to being stretched, pulled, or worked. When we use them in a movement that hasn't occurred we will feel those muscles tensing up. Then, when we actually take time to relax, we feel the pain of irregular movement, and are defeated before we have started the new activity. Athletes train their bodies to perform. They exercise their muscles and force themselves to push beyond what they'd done previously. The same is true of us in our endeavors as Christians.

We become all excited when we see a new opportunity for service. We want to jump in without preparation and get the job done. Our reasoning is faulty and we face many roadblocks along the way. Research on the project must be completed and we must understand the culture we are hoping to impact. Most importantly, we must prepare ourselves mentally and spiritually for the task ahead.

We can do this by maintaining a daily and consistent walk with God. There is no short cut to becoming spiritual giants, strong in faith and determination. It begins by completing smaller tasks faithfully.

The tiny fire is already there just as our muscles are already in our bodies. It takes effort and regular exercise to increase our muscle strength and stamina; and it takes effort and regular exercise to increase our mental and spiritual strength. We need to work our bodies, and put into practice what we learn from our own study and observing others; and we need to surround ourselves with like minded people.

Just as athletes reap the benefit of hard work and exercise, so we, too, will reap the benefit of consciously putting into practice what we already know. Exercise can be painful, but the result is well worth the effort. There is no time to waste! Let's get started today!

Counselors

"The way of a fool seems right to him, but a
wise man listens to advice."
(Proverbs 12:15, NIV)

But in your hearts set apart Christ as Lord.
Always be prepared to give an answer to
everyone who asks you to give the reason for
the hope that you have. But do this with
gentleness and respect. . ."
(1 Peter 3:15, NIV)

For a long time we've known that God has been calling us to do something different. We've been afraid. We'd believed that when God leads, there will be no fear. Somehow, we woke up to realize that we really wouldn't need Him if there was complete and perfect peace every time we made a decision. We've found true courage and have chosen to step out, trusting God to lead the way and to provide for us in spite of the fear. It was incredibly hard to do, but we've done it! We've stepped beyond our fears and left the familiar known as comfort zones. We are confident we've made the right decision and walked into the future, amazed at the goodness of God. He's met us at every turn. But wait! What is that ahead of us? Could it be that we have more difficulties ahead? Why is it that some of those closest to us are standing in the way of our new walk with God? They are godly people, and we know they love us. Then why the hassle?

It is true that God doesn't reveal His will for our lives to everyone around us. However, the above scripture is also important. We must learn to listen to those around us (according to Proverbs 12:15). We must also be careful to have an answer for those closest to us when they question our motivation. Good communication can dispel their concerns and help them to understand how God is directing us. I Peter 3:15 tells us to use gentleness and respect when explaining ourselves. Once they understand what we feel we are called to do, we just might gain some loyal supporters.

We need to think through what we feel God is calling us to do. Then we should talk to the people who are closest to us; having an answer for their questions. We may not be able to satisfy all their questions, but we will have solidified in our own minds what we are going to do. The great thing in all of this is that we have acted according to God's directives for our lives.

M. JOYCE HALVORSON

Dare to be a Daniel

". . . but the people that do know their God
shall be strong, and do exploits."
(Daniel 11:32, KJV)

Have you wanted God to use you, to flow through you, but thought you didn't have the right qualifications? "God can't use me," you've often said, "I have too many strikes against me." Daniel had some major strikes against him as well. He was an exile, a captive. He wasn't free to move around like you or me. He wasn't even in his own country. He, and his fellow countrymen, had been taken captive and moved to Babylon.

Daniel refused to do what everyone else was doing. He refused to eat the delicacies from the King's table. He remained firm in his convictions and wouldn't defile himself. Instead, he put His faith in God on the line, and suggested a trial of vegetables and water for himself and his friends. He followed God's commands and kept himself pure. He continued to pray openly, risking death in a den of lions. God miraculously delivered him. Eventually God gave him dreams and visions that many of us have studied.

What made him so special? Why didn't he give in to the taunts and commands of those around him? He knew his God. He believed, and trusted Him implicitly. There was no doubt in his mind as to whom he was serving. He had nothing going for him and everything against him; when offered success, he chose God's way, and seeming disaster. He refused to bend to an easier way of living. Rejecting popularity and progress, he remained faithful. He wasn't looking for dreams and visions. He was looking for an intimate relationship with his God. He was more interested in what God thought than what those around him were saying. Yet it was this faithfulness that resulted in dreams and visions, and the ability to interpret others' dreams.

Father, may our trust in you be like that of Daniel. May our relationship with you drive us to our knees and to your Word. Create within us a longing, a passion to know you better. Even when we feel as though everything is against us, may our eyes remain on you. Help us, Lord, to be totally caught up with being your child. Cause everything around us to fade away as we learn intimacy with you. Teach us, Father, to be your child.

Calouses

". . . I will remove from them their heart of stone and give them a heart of flesh. Then they will follow my decrees and be careful to keep my laws. They will be my people, and I will be their God."
(Ezekiel 11:19-20, NIV)

A callous generally appears where the skin has had a lot of rubbing. Calluses appear on the hands of labourers and on the bottoms of our feet. A labourer can no longer feel extremes in temperature because of the build up of dead skin. A calloused heart is one that has had some bruising and rubbing. It has lost its ability to feel. There is no emotion because there is no feeling. It has built up a hard, thick wall around it. This wall was not put up intentionally. As each minute injury occurred, scarring also occurred. These, in turn, became calluses. Several calluses united becoming one big callous.

I've had calluses on my feet. One way to remove them is to use a tool resembling a file, scraping dead skin until my feet are smooth again. Sometimes I soak my feet first, allowing the water to soften the hardened areas. Then the scraping is more effective. It's rather ironic, isn't it? Chaffing and repeated rubbing causes calluses. Yet, scraping is required to remove those very calluses. There may not have been a great deal of pain when the calluses were forming, but pain will occur as they are removed.

When we ask God to remove the calluses and give us a heart of flesh, we are asking Him to inflict discomfort and pain. As the calluses are removed from our hearts we will begin to feel. Not only will we feel the comfortable feelings, but we will also be susceptible to pain. The arrow and darts thrown our way in the past could not penetrate the hardness. With the calluses removed, they have the potential to inflict pain. Yet, God has clearly said that we must surrender our calloused hearts to Him, and He will replace them with hearts of flesh.

Knowing that I will feel more pain almost makes me retract that prayer. I also know that unless I allow God to do this necessary heart surgery in me, I will not grow, and will eventually destroy myself. Having considered my options, I choose the heart of flesh. How about you?

Fitness

*"Have nothing to do with godless myths
and old wives' tales; rather, train yourself
to be godly. For physical training is of some
value, but godliness has value for all things,
holding promise for both the present life
and the life to come."*
(I Timothy 4:7&8, NIV)

Calgary, and Airdrie, my home city, are hockey cities. It is fascinating to watch the puck fly around the ice, sometimes hitting hockey players, the plexi glass, or the net. I may understand some of the game, but it won't make me a hockey player. My cycling during the summer months may cause me to become more fit, physically, but that is all. Owning a good quality bicycle will not make me a cyclist on the same level as Lance Armstrong. I have to work at it, training diligently and disciplining my body so that my endurance improves. Occasional spurts of working my body will not work, either. I must be consistent, training my body to become all that I want it to be.

Training means consistent effort in a particular area. It has little to do with arm chair athletes who seem to have all the answers yet do very little beyond critiquing a performance. Training also implies that there has been a coach involved in the athlete's life. As I think of all the people in our church, I am pleased to find spiritual coaches. They have disciplined themselves in godliness; I love to sit and listen to the overcoming stories of their lives.

The Apostle Paul readily admitted the value of physical training. He said that is was of some value. He also stated that training ourselves to be godly was of value both now and throughout eternity. Isn't it odd that people will watch what they eat and avoid harmful activities so that they will be healthy people, yet they fail to apply the same principles to their spiritual lives?

What a different people we would be if we applied the same discipline to our spiritual bodies as we do to our physical bodies. It's mind boggling! Our "athletic performance" would be phenomenal! Paul commanded us to train ourselves to be godly. It's hard work and requires persistence; but it's to our advantage and to the advantage of the hurting people around us. Will you obey the command?

Heart food

"But the Counsellor, the Holy Spirit, whom
the Father will send in my name, will
teach you all things and will remind you of
everything I have said to you."
(John 14:26, NIV)

When my oldest son was in grade one, I would get him ready for school. Before he went out the door, I read Psalm 121 to him. I did this every day for an entire month. By the end of the month he was saying it with me as I read. I'm not sure if he was in a rush to get out the door or if he actually enjoyed it! That's how easy memorizing scripture can be. In this computer age we want everything pre-programmed. We live in such a fast paced world that there is no time for us to slow down enough to do the proper programming. That's what we are doing as we memorize scripture and help our children do the same. That's what we are doing when we allow television and peers influence how our children act and react. Instilling God's Word in our minds and eventually in our hearts is programming our hearts and minds to think a certain way.

Whenever we need some wisdom from God, a verse comes to mind. That's because the Holy Spirit has been assigned to bring all things to our minds -- as we need them. This gives us the basic principle for responding and making decisions the more we have God's Word in our hearts.

Over the years I've heard of all kinds of ways of memorizing and meditating on Scripture. The simplest is just doing it. There is no magical formula. Simply saying it out loud enough times will cement it in our minds. When we need to rely upon it, it will be there for us. Psalm 121 has eight verses in it, and takes less than two minutes to read. Yet it took a five-year-old less than thirty days to repeat it from memory. Some people have photographic memories, can read something once, and have it memorized. Others take longer to accomplish the same task. There is no shame in needing more time to memorize scripture. The shame comes in not doing it. Let's be doers, and memorizers, of the Word. Let's begin today.

> "I have hidden your word in my heart that I might not sin against you."
>
> (Psalm 119:11, NIV)

Extreme Makeovers

"Forget the former things; do not dwell on the past. See, I am doing a new thing! Now it springs up; do you not perceive it: I am making a way in the desert, and streams in the wasteland."
(Isaiah 43:18 & 19, NIV)

I loved the TV show, Extreme Makeover Home Edition with host Ty Pennington. A deserving family who faced adversity or who'd accomplished amazing things with very little would receive a new home—free. Then a mass of people in the construction trades would assemble the dream in under a week. It would contain everything imaginable to make life more bearable.

Extreme makeovers have occurred in the Bible for centuries, with God as the host and head designer. Saul, the worst persecutor of the early church, passionately pursued early Christians, putting them in prison or killing them. God gave him an extreme makeover, and he became Paul, passionately leading those he once enslaved. God enabled him to use his passion to spread the Gospel throughout the known world.

Isaiah foretold extreme makeovers long before Saul became Paul. God was creating a way to go through the driest places, and those places that were unproductive would receive waterways. There had been areas that once were productive, but had become garbage dumps; now nothing grew. Water was sent to them in such abundance that rivers appeared. God is poised, ready to do the same things in our lives.

He is creating paths through the toughest, driest areas of our lives. We have His word that we will go THROUGH that desert. We will, in fact, produce hardy fruit, the kind that will not wilt. It may seem like we are drying up; instead we are changing; fruit is appearing in the unlikeliest places. For those of us who once were productive, God is changing the garbage heaps as well. He is not through with us. We have not been abandoned. He is sending healing, refreshing water to those places we've messed up. It will be such an excessive amount that it will spill out to everyone around us.

God is ready! All He needs is our permission to demolish the crumbling structure of our lives and give us new life. Will you give Him permission?

Eyesight

"Come to me, all you who are weary and
burdened, and I will give you rest."
(Matthew 11:28, NIV)

A friend of mine and her children loved to watch the industrious antics of the beaver colony at work near their property in northern British Columbia. They would remove part of the beaver dam and then through the tall grass they would creep, pushing aside all hindrances that impeded their view. There was one goal in mind: that of seeing the beavers hard at work. The young family was not disappointed. The entire colony, plus some helpers, was out in full force, rebuilding and repairing the breach. It was fascinating to watch until the "head beaver" spotted them. Instantly, all activity ceased and all eager beavers disappeared from sight.

I was thinking about this one Sunday morning as we were singing about wanting to know God and the effort involved in doing so. There are things we must do in order for this to transpire. We are like my friend's family. We sing those prayers and desperately long to be in God's arms. Just like my friend and her children, we begin pushing aside the stuff that impedes our view and prevents us from reaching our goal. But unlike them, we panic! We see Him, and just at the moment that he sees us, we run from his presence, terrified!

He is not afraid of us. He is waiting for us to come, and He will not disappear as we near Him. He will, in fact, reach out to us and draw us into His arms. Neither do we need to fear His presence. He will not reject us. There is never so much baggage that He will send us away. All we need to do is to start recognizing what the barriers between ourselves and God are. That is the beginning of pushing the hindrances aside. Beavers may run from our presence, but God never will. He will do the opposite and run toward us – His arms open wide, ready and eager to receive us.

> "Father, like a child I come – just as I am, dirty and covered in debris. I have nothing of value to give you. Take me as I am, and change my filthy garments for a robe of righteousness."

M. JOYCE HALVORSON

Become

Every morning a native elder from the Peigan tribe burns incense because he believes it will open his way to God. It's a ritual he has performed for many years. He wants to be all that God wants him to be. In a presentation I attended he challenged us to think of one thing that we could do now, today, to initiate change for the better. He formerly worked at a halfway house for natives where he challenged them, that no matter what kind of a life they'd lived, or whatever trouble they were in, to think of one thing they could do right then to begin the change they claimed to want. I left that presentation challenged to live my life as consistently as possible.

An aboriginal elder is not someone who is elected to the position. It is a position that is attained through a consistent, disciplined life. He has been faithful in learning all aspects of his culture and has been found able and qualified to teach others what he believes. In the same way Scripture commands us to become qualified to teach, or to lead others.

I love teaching others, and it has occurred to me that I need to maintain more consistent lifestyle so that I will teach others in the ways of my God. All we need to do is to look in the mirror to discover the first step needed to begin a change. This change needs to happen!

It begins with me and it begins with you. True change begins within us. God is at work. However, the responsibility is not solely His. We must discipline ourselves; and we must develop our relationship with God. That is our responsibility. God is not interested in a church full of robots; He does want a church full of people who are growing closer towards Him and to each other. That will only happen as we become consistent doers of the Word, and not hearers only (James 1:22). We will become doers when we are disciplined and consistent followers of Christ.

Becoming fit

*"Create in me a pure heart, O God, and
renew a steadfast spirit within me."*
(Psalm 51:10, NIV)

Have you wanted to become more fit -- someday? How about being better read? How about a closer relationship with someone you love? Some will only dream about self improvement while others assess the situation, and create a plan of what must be done to reach the desired goal.

Becoming more fit physically requires a great deal of commitment. It begins with just a few minutes of our time, a few times a week. The easiest step is to begin taking short walks, lengthening them every two or three days. Another good idea is to practice good posture going up and down stairs in our homes. A third vital step is to eat healthy food. Cut out the kinds of food that make you feel less than healthy.

Reading good books begins one book at a time, one word at a

time. It really doesn't matter whether we are great readers, fast readers, or slow readers. Just do it at whatever pace is good for you. Each of us is a little different in this area. But what is true for everyone, is that what we put into our minds, and eventually into our hearts, is the way we will think and act.

We all understand that if we want to get to know someone better, we must spend time with them. We need to just "hang out" with them, knowing them when they are practicing their best behaviour and when they're not. Quality time, as the old cliché says, is far more important than quantity time. I disagree. Just being with someone casually often speaks volumes where a couple of hours in an expensive restaurant will tell you very little about how a person thinks.

If we want to become strong, healthy men and women of God, a great worship service with wonderful preaching will not suffice. What will be of infinite value is the time we spend alone with God during the week. We learn to hear His voice as we spend time in His presence. We learn to hear His heartbeat as we read and meditate on His Word. It begins with a few minutes a few times a week, gradually increasing. There is no short cut to knowing God. It takes daily discipline the same way becoming physically fit takes discipline.

I have a dream

"being confident of this, that he who began a good work in you will carry it on to completion until the day of Christ Jesus."
(Philippians 1: 6, NIV)

Do you have a dream or a vision for your life? Are you aware of the gifts God has given you? Very few people do what they do for a living just by chance. They begin their lives with a dream, or vision, of what they'd like to do. Then the planning begins. What is involved in accomplishing their dream, of reaching their goal? For some it will mean several years of education, but for all it means a lot of hard work, at times working long hours for minimum wages. The goal is continually held in sight as we train to be all that we have dreamt.

Nothing with God is haphazard, either. He has a plan. He is certain of that plan and will complete it. Each plan varies according to His purpose or will for our lives. We can choose to co-operate with God's plan or we can attempt to do it ourselves, often with disastrous results. Seldom can we can see the entire plan. Yet, God is leading us and shaping us into the person He wants us to be. He has infinite patience with us, repeating instructions and waiting for us until we follow Him.

God has begun to do amazing things in each of us. Sometimes, however, it feels as though He has abandoned us. Our lives have stalemated. Nothing new has happened in a long time. We've continued doing what we think God wants us to do. Yet, life seems empty and colorless. Work becomes drudgery. What has happened? Nothing. God has not forgotten us. It is at times like this that we need to hang on to the promise that God will complete the work that He has begun. Our responsibility in this is to remain faithful, and to look inside us for pockets of resistance to the will of God. As those faulty areas become evident, we are to deal with them, asking God to clean us of the dirt found there and to fill us again with His power. It is easy to lose the way because God doesn't show us very much further than the next step. But as we remain obedient to Him, He will complete us – in His time.

Believe

"Now to him who is able to do immeasurably more than all we ask or imagine, according to his power that is at work within us . . ."
(Ephesians 3:20, NIV)

Have you dreamed big dreams this week? Has God put within you a vision of what He wants to do through you? Have you begun to believe, with a passion, the dream that seems only a dream? There are some things that you must do so that your dream will come to pass.

1. We must know how to see it and understand it before there is any physical evidence. It takes the eye of faith to see the end result before getting to the end. When Samuel was sent to anoint one of the sons of Jesse as the next king of Israel, God rejected several. Finally, David was presented to Samuel. God chose this one. God didn't see the youthfulness or the lack of worldly experience. He chose to look beyond the obvious and saw a King. What no one else saw, God saw.

2. Frequently, we meet people that do not believe the way we do. They try to dissuade us from the path we have chosen, and may discourage us from holding on to our dream. Satan will attack anything that builds the kingdom of God. He does not have to use the ungodly in this world when he can get Christians to discourage each other. When we believe in what God has put within us, we will function in the same dimension as God functions.

"And without faith it is impossible to please God,"

(Hebrews 11:6, NIV)

3. We must carry within us that dream, carefully nurturing it until its birth. It's much like a baby, conceived and then born. The baby didn't become immediately. It took careful nurturing. If we have truly understood the dream, and seen beyond the obvious and believed in what God has called us to do, we must not allow it to be aborted.

God has big dreams for us, bigger than we could ever imagine. We are so often limited by our senses. We have the capacity to dream big dreams. By faith we can see beyond the darkness of discouragement. Through faith we see the completion of a dream. Do things look impossible? God is bigger than any impossibility. He is God.

M. JOYCE HALVORSON

Achieve the impossible

". . . let us throw off everything that hinders and the sin that so easily entangles, and let us run with perseverance the race marked out for us."
(*Hebrews* 12:1, NIV)

When Joseph was sold into slavery, it looked as though his dreams were merely a figment of his imagination. The difference was that Joseph never lost his dream. He hung on tenaciously and believed that God had spoken to him and had given him a dream. Did he bemoan his fate while in an Egyptian prison? Hardly. He kept himself busy. He knew what needed to be done in order for his dream to mature. He worked hard and found favour with whoever was over him in authority. He gained an audience with Pharaoh, and his dream was given new life. Had he ever lost sight of his dream, he would never have become second in command to Pharaoh. His family would not have survived, and history would be different from the way we know it.

God worked, and he created us to work. His plan is for us to work in order to realize his purposes for our lives. We must develop our abilities and learn to be patient and persistent in following God's agenda. Sometimes the pace is unbearably slow. We want to run ahead and do more. We see the goal and rush toward it. Wait! Our lives and our plans must be continually evaluated in light of God's Word and His dream for our lives. Are we staying on course?

Like Joseph who never lost sight of his dreams, our lives have the same potential when we completely surrender to God's plan for our lives. It is imperative that we follow God's plan. It may seem like the "scenic route" instead of the short cut; but it is never the wrong way. In God's timing we will discover that the seemingly impossible has become a reality. Remember, God's dreams are not for the faint hearted. He is looking for people who are patient and persistent in following their dreams. The work may be hard, and the hours long, but the reward comes to those who wait.

Go ahead! Dream big dreams, God's dreams, and don't lose sight of the goal. Don't quit too soon. Don't get behind. Don't run ahead. Keep pace with God as he works the impossible in your life.

M. JOYCE HALVORSON

Energy conservation

"Do not be anxious about anything, but in everything . . . present your requests to God. And the peace of God, which transcends all understanding, will guard your hearts and your minds in Christ Jesus."
(Philippians 4:6&7)

Remember the time when gas was under 50 cents per liter? Then there was the high cost of natural gas with the monthly bill of $50. Those were the days. . . . With the high cost of energy these days I am sure we are all thinking of ways to conserve energy, and therefore our money. I've signed up for a 5 year fixed rate, and time will tell whether I've made a mistake; but it has evened out how much I will spend for that commodity.

I was laying in bed thinking about other kinds of energy and how much it really takes to do things. For example, it takes a lot of energy to get mad. There is also a huge payout when we are worried about anything, not to mention the high cost of stress.

God understands energy conservation. We have His peace and much more energy when we give Him our burdens and concerns.

It also seems that I have so much more energy when I've invested in someone's life by helping them. It's more than a "warm fuzzy" feeling after such an event. It's a quick return on my investment. Scripture once again reminds us of what we will receive after we've expended our energy in someone's life.

> *"Give, and it will be given to you. . . . For with the measure you use, it will be measured to you."*
>
> *(Luke 6:38, NIV)*

God has promised us an amazing return on our investments, if only we will use what we have to enrich another person's life. He pours his life into ours when we spend our energy in aiding someone else. This leaves us with more get-up-and-go to conduct our daily lives.

Yes, God is in the energy conservation business. He's been there all along. In the busyness of our lives, we consider ways in which we can use our energy more wisely. God's Word is full of advice in this area. It may be a new problem, but it has an old, but relevant, solution. Let's begin today to examine God's Word for other instructions on conserving our energy.

M. JOYCE HALVORSON

The language of excellence

"... For out of the overflow of the heart the mouth speaks."
(Matthew 12:34b, NIV)

I talk to myself all the time. I ask myself a question and then get to answer it. I don't always agree with the answers I get either. Sometimes Holy Spirit has dropped an answer into my mind. My natural mind responds or reacts to it. The end results are often quite challenging. The biggest danger in all this is that I can be guilty of telling myself a lie. That is, I begin with an element of truth, possibly speculating on an unpleasant situation, and then the conversation gets rolling. What we hear ourselves repeating, we soon start believing. We tell ourselves a lie, and then begin to believe it even though we know that it was pure speculation. We have deceived ourselves and have become what we've thought.

The choice to be excellent begins with aligning your thoughts and words with the intention to require more of yourself. (Oprah Winfrey) We pray and ask God to change us. Then we beat ourselves up because we cannot notice any instant changes. We continue to feel as though God has forsaken us.

Are angry words a regular part of our vocabulary? They are generally a symptom of something much deeper within us. What is required is that we deal with the hidden pain in our lives.

God always answers prayer. As we align ourselves with the intent to speak righteous thoughts, the deep inner recesses of our hearts are exposed. God is doing a housecleaning in our lives. He is exposing the dirt (sin). It is our decision to deal with it. Sometimes we must choose to forgive and other times repentance is required. Speaking the language of excellence is an incredible decision each of us is faced with. Many times we will be faced with contradicting statements in our minds. Do we choose to believe, and repeat what the Bible says? Or do we choose to remain in our comfort zones, and therefore sin by allowing incorrect thoughts to captivate us?

Change begins with making a decision to change. It progresses as we continually align our thoughts and words with the Word of God. Then, as the dirt is brought to light, we choose to deal with it, and we have begun to speak the language of excellence.

M. JOYCE HALVORSON

Excellence in training

> *". . . Forgetting what is behind and straining toward what is ahead, I press on toward the goal to win the prize for which God has called me heavenward in Christ Jesus."*
> *(Philippians 3:13-14, NIV)*

I love to watch figure skating. Whenever The Canadian Figure Skating Championships is broadcast, very little was accomplished in my home as I found myself glued to the television. I was fascinated by the fortitude of the participants. They fell down, picked themselves up and carried on. A person would have thought that the routines were learned and that no one would fall. That was not the case as virtually all the participants made some form of mistake. After every fall they had an extremely short memory. The skaters appeared to have forgotten they'd fallen – they simply carried on. The same should be true of us in our walk with God.

We all make mistakes. We fall down, bemoan our poor lot in life, and stoically declare ourselves failures. We know God forgives us. Yet, we refuse to forgive ourselves and try again. It is much easier to say we are failures than to pick ourselves up and carry on. We can try as hard as we want to be perfect and to never make mistakes. But they will happen.

We need to become more like the figure skaters. They would never reach their level of achievement had they surrendered to defeat the first time they fell or were bested by someone else. They used their failure as a tool to do better next time. Failure has been said to be "excellence in training." It proves that, at the very least, we had the courage to try. Then, after falling, we have the back-bone to pick ourselves up and try again.

The journey to excellence begins with a decision to do more or be better than we've done or been before. It continues as we align our thoughts and words with God's will for our lives. Each failure can be the starting point for something excellent. We will become people of excellence as we learn to look ahead, and not behind us, to the final prize.

Let's choose today to live excellent lives.

M. JOYCE HALVORSON

Face the enemy

"Submit yourselves, then, to God. Resist the
devil, and he will flee from you."
(James 4:7, NIV)

"My grace is sufficient for you, for my
power is made perfect in weakness.
Therefore I will boast all the more gladly
about my weaknesses, so that Christ's
power may rest on me. That is why, for
Christ's sake, I delight in weaknesses, in
insults, in hardships, in persecutions, in
difficulties. For when I am weak, then I am
strong."
(2 Corinthians 12: 9, 10, NIV)

The fight is on! In my mind I cannot see what I am fighting. The onslaught has been so fast that I am down under the weight of it before I know what is happening. It usually is thoughts of inferiority or loneliness that threaten to take out any energy I have.

This generally goes on for a while. Then a ray of light shines into my darkness and I am able to put a name to what it is I am fighting. Strangely enough, the battle is won. When I am able to turn around and face the enemy, he runs.

The weapons of spiritual warfare are only effective when we are on the offensive. There is no room to turn and run from our problems. It is only as we face them that we can win the battle.

There are a lot of things that affect how well I do. Among them are how tired I am or if I've been ill. In facing our enemy, whatever it is, we must ask God to show us what it is that we are fighting. It's frightening to ask this, but even more so to continue on, feeling as though our emotional and mental well being are being threatened by some unknown force. There are times when I've known that the enemy of our souls is behind the attack, but I lack the strength to resist. It is in those weakest times that God comes and delivers.

When I get all upset that I lack the ability to resist the enemy as we are instructed to, I am reminded that it is God's strength working in me that does the resisting. My responsibility is the willingness to face the enemy. It can be the hardest thing I have ever done. It would certainly be easier to succumb to the pressure, to lie down and submit to wrong thoughts. But I have learned over the years that comfort and security come in relying on God's strength and fighting the good fight of faith.

M. JOYCE HALVORSON

Clear away the clutter

> *"Therefore, since we are surrounded by such a great cloud of witnesses, let us throw off everything that hinders and the sin that so easily entangles, and let us run with perseverance the race marked out for us."*
> (Hebrews 12:1, NIV)

I gave away my hide-a-bed. I'd tried to sell it, but to no avail. So I gave it to someone who needed it. The hide-a-bed was in very good condition, but it was in the way of simplifying my life. If I couldn't sell something I gave it away, threw it away, or took it to the recycle depot. My junk could be someone else's treasures. It's taken a great deal of effort to sort through things I once thought irreplaceable, and the task is by no means complete. But, slowly, my life is becoming uncluttered.

I couldn't help but notice the parallel between uncluttering my life and the process we go through in our quest for a more intimate relationship with the Lord. Many times we talk about getting rid of sin as the best way to a closer walk with God.

We insist that focusing all our attention on Jesus will most certainly get us to the finish line. We are right, to a point. However, there are other processes we must go through as well.

There are decisions made in simplifying our lives that can be more painful than turning our back on sin. Sometimes we are involved in too much activity. There may be nothing wrong with what we are doing. It's just that we are doing too much. We work at our jobs, sing, teach, preach, and serve others. At the end of the day we fall into bed too exhausted to pray. In the morning we are up and running, thus repeating the vicious cycle. Our intentions are honorable, but we've lost sight of our main purpose in life, that of glorifying God. God wants us to balance our activity for Him and a relationship with Him. He has not called us to a life of busyness; He's called us to a life of relationship with Him. He wants us to enjoy everything He's given to us, not merely mistaking busyness for relationship. We are meant to enjoy His blessing on our lives.

Let's begin today by taking a hard look at the clutter in our lives. Could it be that there is just too much stuff? Have we over-committed ourselves to the point of burning out? Let's begin today to clear away the clutter.

M. JOYCE HALVORSON

The darkest valley

"Even though I walk through the valley of the shadow of death (or darkest valley), I will fear no evil, for you are with me; your rod and your staff, they comfort me."
(Psalm 23:4, NIV)

My home town has miles and miles of pathways for walkers, cyclist and whoever else appreciates the outdoors. Some of them are on top of a burm while others skirt businesses or residential neighborhoods. The path from the RCMP building to the walkway across the highway is a frequently used path. I take my bike over it during the summer and walk to friends' homes, or the swimming pool. Most of the time I have no problem walking along its paved length; the back yards of many creative Airdrie residents can be viewed as one progresses towards the overpass and beyond. However, I do not like using that path after dark; I can't see far enough in front of me for safety. Before the new fence was erected, some light was able to filter through; but now there is nothing but blackness. One never knows whether danger is lurking in the shadows! I was reading Psalm 23 this week and found an interesting parallel.

Sometimes we find ourselves in some incredibly difficult circumstances. We are not sure what we should do; nothing makes sense and there is no logical direction laid out in front of us. We are scared! What will happen next? Fences are erected to keep out the danger; but they also become light blockers. Previous sources of wisdom and strength are unable to reach us and the darkness around us becomes blacker. The Psalmist did not stop at the darkness, however. He said that he found himself in difficult or dangerous circumstances; he did not fear the darkness because God was with Him, protecting him and comforting him. Isn't that amazing?

Like David, who'd had to endure trials and difficulties, and found comfort and strength in God's presence, so we can find safety and strength there as well. He is always with us; all we need to do is ask for His help. It may involve dismantling fences we've erected for our own protection, and it may mean facing danger head on. Just remember God has said that He will never leave us alone. We have His Word on that!

Honest to each other

". . . be transformed by the renewing of your mind."
(Romans 12:2, NIV)

In 2 Corinthians, the Apostle Paul reminds the church at Corinth of his reasons for being hard on them in a previous letter. He urges them to love one another and to forgive those who have offended them. He then reminds them of his love for them and relates how painful it was for him to be so stern with them. He uses the phrase,

"as surely as the truth of Christ is in me"

(2 Corinthians 11:10, NIV)

He then explains that it is because of this truth that he is able to succeed. Paul obeyed God implicitly. The same ought to be true for us as well.

We love to use Zechariah 8:16 when we tear a fellow Christian apart.

"These are the things you are to do: Speak the truth to each other, and render true and sound judgment in your courts."

(Zechariah 8:16, NIV)

We think we are only obeying what God has spoken to us about. But before we go to another person with a message that could hurt them, we should use the following as a safety check:

1.Does this message really apply to the person I want to speak with? Or does it apply to my life? Frequently when we see a fault in another person, we are merely looking in the mirror.

2.Is it really necessary? It could be that God is already at work, and any involvement on our part might slow the process. God may have intended our insight/word of knowledge to be used as a prayer guide.

3.Is my heart right with God? Have I spent time with the Lord concerning the message He has given me?

4.Am I able to speak the truth in love?

This is not an all inclusive list. However, it does bring our attention to what really matters. We are to love each other unconditionally, and we are also to be honest and open with each other. We are not to be as the proverbial bull in a china shop whenever we receive a word from God. Once we have examined our own hearts on the matter in question we are to "speak the truth in love". When we have done this we will have assisted our fellow believer on his/her journey to the renewal of their mind.

Honest to God

". . . Do not think of yourself more highly than you ought, but rather think of yourself with sober judgment, . . . just as each of us has one body with many members, and these members do not all have the same function, so in Christ we who are many form one body, and each member belongs to all the others."
(Romans 12:3, NIV)

The rest of that passage goes on to describe parts of the spiritual body, emphasizing our differences. Each of us has a gift unique to whom we are. When God made us, he placed within us special talents and abilities. Individually, we are the only person that can fulfil those talents correctly. We are unique, and yes, we are different. God is a God of diversity. He loves variety!

Our physical bodies are made of a myriad of parts, each of which is vital to the proper functioning of the body. In the same way the Body of Christ is put together. We have a variety of talents and abilities. Each is necessary to the correct functioning of the body. We are so important to the rest of the body that, without our involvement, the Body of Christ would be handicapped. No matter how small or insignificant we may think we are, we are a vital part.

We must accurately assess our abilities in the Body of Christ. We need to be honest with ourselves, and with God. What am I capable of doing? What is the truth in this situation? What are the lies? Here again, Satan would love to get us believing a lie, and doubt our self worth. We are led to believe that because we are not the same as someone else, we are of no value to the body. The picture is distorted and we cannot see the truth for what it is. Once again, the enemy of our souls has won. He has successfully manipulated us into believing we are worthless.

Renounce the lies, acknowledge the truth. Accurately, and honestly, assess your strengths and weaknesses. Reaffirm yourself. Know that our God does not make mistakes. He has a very special place for each one of us in His Body. We may not be perfect, but we are loved and of great value to our maker. He has begun a process in us, and he will complete it -- in His time.

Honest – to me

"...be transformed by the renewing of your mind..."
(Romans 12:2, NIV)

"True instruction was in his mouth and nothing false was found on his lips..."
(Malachi 2:6, NIV)

The story was told of a traveling salesman who had been away from home for a while. It was getting late in the evening on a cold winter night. High drifts lined the country road. The man was driving slowly along when his car became stuck in a snow drift. Repeated attempts at rocking the car out of the drift failed, so he started walking. A lighted window was seen in the distance and he headed towards it. As he trudged along, he began to think that the farmer would probably be too cold to go out once again. He likely wouldn't trust strangers anyways. By the time the salesman arrived at the house, he'd erroneously arrived at the conclusion that no one would help him. When the door was opened with an offer of help, he yelled, "You can keep your tractor and your shovel! I don't need them!"

I really don't know if that actually happened. However, it does illustrate the point that we frequently tell ourselves fictitious stories based upon inaccurate information. We tell ourselves that if this .... were true, then that ......also must be true – and so the damage is done. What was probably said, or done, in innocence has now become an injury. We then begin to mete out criticism in an effort to justify ourselves, or we begin to whip ourselves because of a perceived lack of perfection in our lives.

One dictionary definition of honest is free from fraud, and the definition of truth is conformity to fact or reality. The salesman in our story did not conform to fact. He allowed himself to become distracted and deceived by fraudulent thoughts. Instead of focusing on his good fortune in finding someone home, he began to think of all the reasons why he would not get the help he needed.

Sometimes a misunderstanding can leave the door open to hurts; but when we look for the truth in a situation and when we refuse to believe anything but the truth, no matter how tempting it may be to do otherwise, we are well on the way to the transformation of our minds.

M. JOYCE HALVORSON

Honestly! – part 1

". . . be transformed by the renewing of your mind."
(Romans 12:2, NIV)

" . . .Do not think of yourself more highly than you ought, but rather think of yourself with sober judgment, in accordance with the measure of faith God has given you."
(Romans 12:3, NIV)

Later on in the same chapter we are reminded that we are all individuals, each of us differing in our talents and abilities.

I really like Romans 12:3 because it instructs me to be honest with myself, and begs questions such as, what am I gifted in? Where do I think God is leading me? It allows me to dream dreams that consider God's call on my life. The challenge, of course, is to be honest with myself, and to not get an unrealistic view of myself.

Arrogance is also known as overconfidence and just being too full of oneself. We get carried away with our dreams and forget about the true Dream Giver. It is God who has made us; we had nothing to do with it. It is very easy for me, for example, to think I've written some pretty good articles and done some awesome things. That may be true, but it is God who has given me the ability to do what I do. I had no say in how He put me together. But, forgetting that God is the source of all things, I could easily become vain and conceited in the way I approach any writing – that would be thinking much more highly than I ought to think.

Sometimes our dreams take us in the wrong direction, down a path we are not meant to walk. Let's be realistic about what we can do. Can we draw a picture? Artists spend a great deal of time developing their skill. Do we have musical abilities? That takes time and work to develop those talents as well. Whatever it is, we cannot develop a talent that is just not there. It is interesting, that as we actively pursue a deeper, more intimate relationship with God, what we really are capable of is what we want to do. Our longings, dreams and aspirations, are placed within us by the Holy Spirit. We will become aware of what He has called us, and not called us to do, as we spend time with God, our talent giver.

Honestly! – part 2

". . . be transformed by the renewing of your mind. . . ," . . . Do not think of yourself more highly than you ought, but rather think of yourself with sober judgment, in accordance with the measure of faith God has given you."

(Romans 12:2-3, NIV)

In the previous story we talked about becoming arrogant when assessing what we are capable of. We recognized that God places talents and abilities within each of us, and that we cannot develop a talent that simply isn't resident within us.

The opposite is also very true. Whenever an article, or sewing project, or anything else, doesn't reach its desired goal, I can allow myself to be devastated and give up entirely, or I can look at the project and see if I can improve my serve (thank you, Chuck Swindoll). Why did this project fail? Is there something I could do different the next time? It's hard to think coherently after a failed effort, but it is so necessary. When God gives us gifts, He expects us to develop them. We do what we think we can do, and maybe fall. But we must pick ourselves up and assess the situation. What can we do differently? Was our timing off? Maybe the project is still salvageable?

Regardless of what has transpired, the fact still remains. We must be honest with ourselves. A job well done deserves a pat on our own backs. I am continually challenged to develop my talents and abilities. I dream of the day when I am actually doing more because of these. All my dreams require my participation or they will remain dreams and never become a goal. Did something go well? Can I do better? We are human beings and learn by doing. God knows this and is waiting for us to come to him. I have dreams about what I would like to do. Hopefully, they are part of God's plan for my life. The only way I will know is by spending time with God and time and effort in working on improving what I've already done, and the same is true for everyone.

It is when we recognize our own value that we will begin on our journey to a transformed and renewed mind. Let's begin the journey today. Let's be honest with ourselves.

$\mathcal{J}$-0-$\mathcal{Y}$

"For the kingdom of God is not a matter of
eating and drinking, but of righteousness,
peace and joy in the Holy Spirit,"
(Romans 14:17, NIV)

Joy is a small word; there are only three letters in it. Yet, without it we are lost, and have great trouble functioning in our day to day lives. Life becomes drudgery as we slog out our existence in a friendless world. There are three key ingredients in having real joy.

J-esus - True joy must begin with our relationship with Jesus Christ. We get to know someone by spending time with them. The more we spend time reading the Bible, the more we will know God. We must also talk with Him. Most of us understand that we present our requests to God when we pray. However, what we fail to realize is that we must also listen to His voice as He speaks to us. God speaks to us in a variety of ways, sometimes in a quiet voice within us, and sometimes through other people.

O-thers - Dale Carnegie, author of *How to Win Friends and Influence People*, said that you can make more friends in two months by becoming interested in other people than you can in two years by trying to get other people interested in you. Having an authentic interest in other people is the second ingredient in having true joy. We must be interested in fellow Christians as well as those who are not. Evangelism must never be the sole basis for friendships, but they do function together. Because we are interested in other people, we will want to tell them about Jesus.

Y –ou – Most of us tend to fall down when it comes to the final ingredient in the recipe for real joy. What matters to us as individuals is very important in finding real joy. As someone so aptly pointed out, " If you don't take care of yourself, then all you have is jo and not joy." We are as incomplete as "jo" when we neglect to care for ourselves.

Knowing Jesus in an intimate way, having an authentic interest in other people, and taking care of ourselves in a balanced lifestyle will bring us true and lasting joy. God designed us to be balanced people, and we will develop true joy as we learn to care for ourselves.

Captivating thoughts

*"Satan rose up against Israel and incited
David to take a census of Israel."*
(1 Chronicles 21:1, NIV)

*"We demolish arguments and every
pretension that sets itself up against the
knowledge of God, and we take captive
every thought to make it obedient to
Christ."*
(2 Corinthians 10:5, NIV)

King David blew it! He was king over all Israel and had victorious forages in enemy territory. Then one day he decided to find out how many fighting men there were in Israel. He had become so obsessed with this idea that he refused to listen to those around him.

The commander of the troops did not like the idea at all because he knew that it would be against God's commands. He tried reasoning with David, but to no avail. The count was made, and God judged them for it. Was this a new thought to David? Did he impulsively make this decision? Probably not. Most often decisions are made after some thought. We sleep on it, stew about it, check it out with friends, and, hopefully, pray about it. Had David checked his thoughts with what the Lord would say, he would have known the answer to be no!

Satan's constant goal is to invade our thoughts and plant his thoughts in our minds. He wants us to believe that what he says is the truth. If he can accomplish this, he has effectively destroyed us. It is impossible to tell where all our thought come from – the TV, our imaginations, memories, or the enemy of our souls.

It is our responsibility to choose the right way, the only way, God's way. It is our responsibility to reject the wrong and embrace the right. We must be continually on guard, monitoring our thoughts. Is what we are thinking in line with the Word? Are we giving God glory in our thoughts? Are we allowing Satan a foothold in our minds, and therefore in our lives? We must remember that the more our thoughts are incorrect, the more space the enemy has to move in and gain control. Conversely, the more our thoughts are right, and true, the more we will be God-honoring and God glorifying people. The choice is ours!

M. JOYCE HALVORSON

Just Lovely

Finally, brothers, whatever is true,
whatever is noble, whatever is right,
whatever is pure, whatever is lovely,
whatever is admirable—if anything is
excellent or praiseworthy—think about
such things.
(Philippians 4:8, NIV)

I work with a person whose favorite expression is "that's just lovely". Most of the time it is meant in a sarcastic manner, while at other times, it's meant the same as, "Wow! That's awesome". Sometimes I will tell her about something positive that's happened, to which she'll reply, "That's just lovely!"

Anger and resentment are like a cancer. They devour our spirits like a beast whose appetite cannot be quenched. Not only does the original offence become much worse than it was initially, the negative impact is felt in great shudders throughout our lives, impacting our bodies, relationships, and everyone around us. That is why the Bible instructs us to deal quickly with the hurtful negative situations in our lives. It is not as though we are to deny anything bad has ever happened to us. We are to acknowledge the hurt and the pain. Then we are to deal with it, forgiving the offender. Once that has been accomplished, we are to remind ourselves that the offence has been taken care of. Dwelling on the pain will only serve to deepen the wound. Failing to correctly deal with wounding will eventually cause physical breakdowns. Thinking about, meditating on, or dwelling on, the pain in our lives will eventually produce a bountiful harvest of sleepless nights and poor health. In the same way, thinking about the good things of life will produce a bountiful harvest of peace and joy. It may even improve our physical health.

All God's promises have conditions. i.e. if you will do... I will do.... The commands such as are found in Philippians have amazing consequences as well.

> *". . . and the God of peace shall be with you."*

> *(Philippians 4:9, NIV)*

When we bring ourselves under the authority of scripture, we have all of Heaven working on our behalf. Think on lovely things, those things that are positive and uplifting. They will produce more energy and excitement, and will loosen the creative forces in our lives allowing us to accomplish awesome deeds. Any athlete can attest to the fact that positive results come from the hard work of training his or her body. In the same way, the exhausting work of disciplining our thoughts will have amazing results -- all because we've been obedient to God's Word in our lives.

M. JOYCE HALVORSON

Learn to listen —
part 1

"Then, because so many people were coming and going that they did not even have a chance to eat, he said to them, 'Come with me by yourselves to a quiet place and get some rest.'"
(Mark 6:31, NIV)

Some people love to go and go and go. Their proverbial candle is burning at both ends, and somehow they've found a wick in the middle which was promptly lit as well. Sometimes it seems we have no choice in the matter; at other times it is entirely our doing. We've made ourselves busy, and then wonder why we are so tired. I tend to tire easily, and when I'm tired, my brain tends to shut down and my skill level looks for the nearest window so it can perform a hasty exit. I feel completely incompetent during times like this, but found encouragement in an example Jesus set for his disciples. They'd been extremely busy as well; they hadn't eaten for a while and there was no time to rest. Jesus knew the importance of rest, and he knew his disciples needed some time alone, so he looked for ways to provide these breaks.

The same holds true for us today. Jesus knows how much we can handle; He does not expect us to wear ourselves out working for him. He wants us to get enough rest. Sometimes, in our love for Jesus and the people around us, we try to do too much, stretching ourselves to the limits of endurance. Then we wonder why God seems so far away. It's not that He's moved, and not necessarily true that we've done anything wrong in itself. It's just that we're tired. I have found in the last little while that God speaks to me all the time; but when I've taken time for myself, caring for me, that the still small voice is much more recognizable.

God designed us as triune beings, spirit, soul, and body; all are important. When we neglect our bodies, the other areas will suffer the consequences. But when we take care of our bodies, our spirits and our souls will soar. It's amazing how much better our spiritual and physical lives will be when we take better care of ourselves.

M. JOYCE HALVORSON

Learn to listen – part 2

"... but many who saw them leaving ... got there ahead of them. ... by this time it was late in the day... send the people away so they can go buy themselves something to eat."

(Mark 6: 31-36, NIV)

The previous story emphasizes the importance of physical rest in hearing God speak to us. Jesus knew its importance and the value it played in the lives of his disciples. He took them away to what he thought was a quiet place. Those lucky men got a little time alone – but was it enough?

They really hadn't been able to get very much rest. They knew Jesus, and they'd spent extended periods of time with Him. This story concludes with feeding 5 thousand people and then ending up with leftovers. Once again Jesus sent them off alone. He knew they still needed time to regroup.

Just like the disciples were called upon in their weariness to extend themselves even further, so sometimes we must do something extra that we did not have the strength in ourselves to do. It is in those times that we receive supernatural energy to complete the task in front of us. However, it is important to note that this is the exception to the rule, and not the rule. In a quick perusal of the Gospels, there are many times when Jesus tried to remain anonymous, not calling attention to himself. He was continually looking for ways to catch some rest. He paced himself, and so must we. The best thing we can do for ourselves, for our church, and for the world around us, is to take care of ourselves, and see to it that we receive sufficient rest. We are able to function on adrenalin for quite a while; mentally and emotionally, we can make it look like God has called us. But then we crash, thinking God has deserted us or that the world and the devil are out to get us, when all that is wrong is that we've neglected to care for ourselves. Each of us has a different energy level, and it is our responsibility to function within that space. It's amazing how much brighter the world appears, and how much clearer God's voice sounds, when we've taken time out to care for our bodies.

M. JOYCE HALVORSON

A level playing field

> "They tie up heavy loads and put them on
> men's shoulders, but they themselves are
> not willing to lift a finger to move them.
> Everything they do is done for men to see:
> ..."
>
> (Matthew 23:4-5, NIV)

Are you a people watcher? Have you ever just sat and watched people as they walked by? Some are dressed very nicely (according to our personal standards) while others appear to have dressed out of someone's rag bag. We tend to pull our shoulders back and sniff as these people pass. "Thank God, that's not us! We're better than that!" a sense of false righteousness is ours when we see someone engaged in an activity not meeting our high standards.

The Pharisees said the same sort of thing. They were proud that they were above the common folk of their day. They never allowed themselves to become dirty (defiled in those days) by touching anything or anyone beneath them. They had a long list of do's and don'ts which was impossible to keep. They loved to be treated as someone special. The places of honour were meant for them. The keeping of the law was impossible. They knew that. It made them look even better when someone was crushed by the burden of guilt. Not once would they help lift the heavy load. These people thought themselves far above the rest of the crowd. They were hypocrites in all they did.

The same holds true for us today. Whenever we assume ourselves to be better than anyone else, we are putting ourselves in the same position as the Pharisees. We are no better than anyone around us. Many of us have already experienced God's transforming power in our lives. Some have yet to receive it. In God's eyes we are all on the same level ground. He loves no one better than any other. He loves no one any less. There is nothing we could do to change this. It is the way He planned for it to be. He wanted us all to come the same way -- through the cross. It is at the foot of the cross where we all must meet. It is where we leave all our burdens, and all our sin. Here is the level playing field. All are on it. All must come by way of the cross.

M. JOYCE HALVORSON

Life can be scary!

"Therefore put on the full armor of God, so that when the day of evil comes, you may be able to stand your ground, and after you have done everything, to stand."
(Ephesians 6:13, NIV)

I once heard a sermon about the difficult path to salvation. We heard that it takes courage to find our salvation. So many times God requires a step of faith from us before we see something change. Like the Israelites fleeing from the Egyptian armies, we can be convinced that there is no way out of our situation. Our enemies are all around us and we will surely see death! It takes fortitude to stand firm and resolve to do nothing when what we really want to do is disappear. The future can be scary when all we can see is the edge of the next step in front of us. Yet that is where we must head.

I am excited because God spoke to me through that sermon. I had already made some decisions regarding my future and I felt

God confirming the path I'd chosen. I had no reason to make the decisions I'd made; I just made them.

The future can look bleak for many of us. I am encouraged to know there are others walking similar paths. They've made tough decisions and they've carried on; sometimes they've done nothing and just stood still. They continue to stand still, or to remain firm in their resolve to follow God.

I am sad to hear of difficult situations, but encouraged at the same time when I've heard the testimonies of how God is meeting needs or helping someone stand tall in the middle of difficulty.

I find it interesting that this scripture assumes that troubles will come just because they come; we must be prepared for them. According to this verse we must put on, or actively use, God's armor. His armor is not what we normally think of as being armor. Further in the same chapter we learn that His armor is meant for use in offensive strategies. The enemy cannot destroy us when we are prepared to face him.

Let's be prepared; let's ask God what His armor will look like in each of our lives. He will show us – we must be ready for His answer.

Living on the edge

> *".....My grace is sufficient for you, for my power is made perfect in weakness'. Therefore I will boast all the more gladly about my weaknesses, so that Christ's power may rest on me.........For when I am weak, then I am strong"*
>
> *(2 Corinthians 12: 9&10, NIV)*

Have you ever wondered how much weight a single piece of paper can hold when it is on its edge? A single sheet of paper, no matter how perfect and clean it may be, cannot hold a thing! But when that same paper is torn into eight equal size pieces and bound together, they can hold a little more. When several sheets of paper are similarly torn, bound together with an elastic band and placed on edge, the original perfect piece of paper can now hold a pen or other similar object, and more. Individually, the paper was quite useless on its own; but when bound together with other torn paper, an amazing strength is realized.

As Christians there may not have been a lot that has interrupted our plans for godly living. This can change quickly, and our lives become torn and ripped apart. The pain becomes unbearable; in agony we cry out to God to take the pain away. We become like Job,

"Night pierces my bones; my gnawing pains never rest."

(Job 30:17, NIV)

We firmly stand on God's Word, unwilling to accept what has happened to us. Yet, the pain and tearing apart continues. We meet others who have similar stories of pain. They, too, have been torn apart; pain has been their companion. As we share our stories with one another, we find a common bond – God has brought us through extreme difficulty. The pain and testimonies of God's deliverance has brought us together. We are bound together by the Holy Spirit, and together we come to an understanding of peace that only God can bring.

We may have been living a good and life before God, but just like the pieces of torn paper bonded together, our effectiveness has been increased immeasurably because of the brokenness and subsequent friendships that have developed. Just like the single sheet of paper, we are ineffective when we are on edge. We become stronger as we allow our lives to be rearranged in the order God has designed for us. Let's allow ourselves to truly live on the edge.

M. JOYCE HALVORSON

The joy of being lopsided

> "I consider everything a loss compared to
> the surpassing greatness of knowing Christ
> Jesus my Lord, for whose sake I have lost all
> things. I consider them rubbish that I may
> gain Christ. ... One thing I do: Forgetting
> what is behind and straining toward what
> is ahead, I press on toward the goal to win
> the prize for which God has called me
> heavenward in Christ Jesus."
> (Philippians 3:8, 13-14, NIV)

Have you ever watched a race? Trained athletes all arrive at the starting line. The gun is fired, and the race is on! Those athletes in the lead become strangely lop-sided as they near the finish line. They run almost parallel to the ground in an effort to have part of their body cross the finish line first. They have become so focused on the goal that all else is forgotten. If we were to talk to these athletes, we would discover similarities in their stories. All have had to focus and re-focus their lives. Viable options have been considered and discarded by their coaches. They haven't always understood. Yet, they've followed instructions. Now, they successfully crossed the finish line.

The same is true for us as Christians. We are focused on completing the race of life. Along the way, there have been many viable options. We've carefully considered them, and perhaps, even tried some of them. They've been great. Yet, our coach has asked us to set them aside, one after another. We haven't understood, and probably even complained about it. "But, we're successful! And fruitful!" we remind the Lord. But God in His infinite wisdom can see further down the road than us and asks us to once again set something aside.

Sometimes we fear losing our balance. Are we not to be whole people, and well-balanced? We have become out of shape – so focused on the goal, that our Coach's orders become a joy. We have become centered on one thing. Our fruitfulness in that one area has become phenomenal!

With hindsight we can see that we have become out of balance, and our perspective seems "off". But the incredible joy and peace that permeates every area of our being has been well worth the cost. We are almost at the finish line! Have we run a good race?

On my knees in the river!

"He that believeth on me, as the scripture hath said, out of his belly shall flow rivers of living water."
(John 7:38, KJV)

In Ezekiel's vision (Ezekiel 47: 1-5), there was an incredible river of water flowing out from the rebuilt temple. There were four measures taken of the depth of this river. The first was ankle deep. This is a picture of us walking in the Spirit. The second measurement was knee deep. When we contrast this with our life in the Holy Spirit, we are reminded of a life of prayer and obedience.

I've often joked about the reason for arthritis in my knees was that I spent so much time on them when my sons were growing up, and now those knees are wearing out! That likely isn't true, but what is true is that a life that has rivers of water flowing from deep within is a life that has learned how to pray. Scripture is filled with examples of people praying. When Ezra realized how far from God the Israelites had strayed, he prayed; and Elijah prayed as he waited for God to send rain. Scripture does not record their specific prayers, but we know they prayed. Just as these great men of God prayed, so we must develop a life spent in prayer. Just like a well exercised joint cannot remain stiff, so it is impossible to remain stiff before God when we truly pray and intercede for the needs around us.

The other reminder is that of obedience. To bow the knee, in many cultures, is to show respect and obedience. It symbolizes the supremacy of the one before whom we bow; literally, they are now higher, or of much more importance than we. In the context of the above verse, we are acknowledging the supremacy of the Holy Spirit in our lives. Jesus prayed, *"Not my will, but thine be done"*. In the same way we must also pray, and not only pray, but act on what the Holy Spirit is asking us to do. Nowhere in scripture does it say that we have to agree with what we are asked to do – we just need to do it. The words of an old hymn come to mind: Trust and obey, for there's no other way to be happy in Jesus, but to trust and obey.

Hip waders

"He that believeth on me, as the scripture hath said, out of his belly shall flow rivers of living water."
(John 7:38, KJV)

Some avid fishermen like to really get into what they do, namely the river. They wear what is commonly called hip waders. They have these ridiculous looking things on as they slowly make their way into deeper water. The fishing is better there, I've been told.

In Ezekiel's vision (Ezekiel 47: 1-5), there was an incredible river of water flowing out from the rebuilt temple. There were four measures taken of the depth of this river. The first was ankle deep. This is a picture of us walking in the Spirit. The second measurement was knee deep, symbolizing a life of prayer, obedience and self denial. The third measurement was taken and found to be to the hips. I thought this was an interesting parallel between hip waders and Ezekiel's vision. Seems to me that it would be a lot of work to stay upright in a flowing river if I was in it up to my hips!

Other translations have rendered the word, hips, as loins, thus signifying reproduction. As we mature as Christians we are invited to go deeper into the river of the Holy Spirit. The river of the Holy Spirit within us will cause us to lead others to God, thus reproducing new life and enlarging God's family. A baby is carried deep within his mother's body until the time for deliverance. In the same way, the river that will flow out of our bellies or inner most beings will do so as we are faithful to do all that the Holy Spirit prompts us to do. It comes from somewhere so deep within us that it is not visible. We can only see the evidence of it.

Songs have been written about the joy of holding a new born baby. It brings the family immeasurable joy and pride. In the same way, whenever any of us have been so honored to bring a new life (new Christian) into the family of God, there is an incredible sense of joy. Watching these same people do as we have done and bring still others into the family give us a deep sense of satisfaction. We have done what God has wanted us to do and reproduced that life so deep within us.

Swimming in the river

"He that believeth on me, as the scripture hath said, out of his belly shall flow rivers of living water."
(John 7:38, KJV)

I can barely swim and I most certainly have never gone swimming in a river. On occasion, I have heard of people who have swum across the English Channel or some other large body of water. What all swimmers have in common, whether they are successful in their swim or not, is physical fitness. Swimmers could not possibly attempt such a feat without careful preparation and repeated exercise. Yet even with all the training and fitness, these swimmers are carried along by the currents and force of the water.

In Ezekiel's vision (Ezekiel 47) there were 4 depth measurements taken in the river flowing out of the temple; ankle deep, knee deep, hip deep, and finally, immeasurably deep. What we need to remember is that this river is flowing. Scripture indicates that this river cannot be crossed. In other words, there is no end to it.

Likewise, the Holy Spirit within us is not in short supply and will never run dry. The Holy Spirit at work is beyond our understanding. Yet, we are to abandon ourselves to the Holy Spirit's direction in our lives. We are to flow in the moving of the Holy Spirit and allow it to carry us along. God, through the Holy Spirit, is directing each movement and activity in our lives. We are simply to maintain our intimacy with Him. As we pray, we hear his voice and then obey his commands.

Just as only the well disciplined are able to survive in the English Channel, so it is in the spirit world. We discipline ourselves to read and study the Bible. Then we discipline ourselves to spend time in prayer and listening for that still small voice giving us direction and teaching us. We are able to accomplish whatever we are instructed to do because we are strong. We've exercised our spirit man and know we can do all things through Him who gives us strength. It is invigorating and challenging. We set out to do what we do not understand nor feel we are capable of. Yet, we do not fear what lies ahead because we have learned to swim in the river.

Bustin' out

*". . . 'Jerusalem will be a city without walls
because of the great number of men and
livestock in it. I myself will be a wall of fire
around it,' declares the Lord, 'and I will be
its glory within.'"*
(Zechariah 2:4&5, NIV)

The Israelites had been decimated; their livestock taken, and women and children removed and placed in captivity. Virtually anything of value had been taken and the Temple destroyed. All hope was gone. Along came a prophet with a message of hope – hope with conditions attached! God's chosen people had gone their own way, incorporating and participating in the evil practices around them. He'd warned them of the consequences of their behavior, but they wouldn't listen. He still loved them. Now God said that if they'd repent, turn around and listen to His voice, He would gather them and bless them beyond their previous state of prosperity. That was the key—repentance and obedience. They would not be able to contain their blessings within the confines of their city! The walls that had been built as protection against marauders would not be able to contain them! But God said that He would protect them and live among them!

In much the same way, many of us have been decimated. It seems as though anything we thought was of value is gone. Our hope has been destroyed! Yet, along comes the promise of redemption, renewal, and restoration. God wants to bless us beyond what we previously experienced. This, too, is a promise with a condition. We must do an "about face", turning our backs on disobedience and our own willfulness. Then we will once again know peace and joy.

But there is more! When God has restored us, we must be prepared for changes! Our previous boundaries and walls built for our own protection and safety will not be able to contain the blessings. They will be insufficient and must be removed. But we will not need to worry because God has promised to be the new wall. He will be around us, among us, and in us. He will live with us! Imagine that – God, so close that we can whisper and He will hear us. We will talk with Him just like we talk with a friend. With all this in our future, we must remember that change is inevitable. We will be bustin' out!

M. JOYCE HALVORSON

Moving on

"And I will put my Spirit in you and move
you to follow my decrees and be careful to
keep my laws."
(Ezekiel 37:27, NIV)

Mom and dad have moved. They've been living in the same house for 19 years, and now they've decided it's time to move on. They took a long time to make the decision, but that was only the beginning! Most of their furniture would have to go, as would two garage sales worth of knick knacks and other assorted items. It was a lot of work, sorting through accumulated memories, and it wasn't easy letting go of years of treasures, each one reminding them of a time, place, or person. However, the gargantuan task was completed in time, and their home was vacated in preparation for moving on.

This is so like us as Christians. We have lived in the same place for a long time. We've accumulated a lot of baggage along the way, some of it healthy mementos of successful projects, and others mementos of things best forgotten, for we've held on to hurts, pain, and frustrations instead of letting go. At times we've wondered whether it is the Holy Spirit's voice we hear or whether Satan is trying to confuse us. We are becoming restless with what we've always known. It's always worked in the past. Why, we even have the proof in our mementos and testimonies.

It's hard to understand the necessity for change, but God is not a static God. He is constantly changing and doing new and different things, and He wants us to move with Him. Scary territory will be encountered along the way, but the Holy Spirit marches on. He is leading us to a new project, one that only we can do.

It is God who put desires in our hearts, and it is He who will begin the tug and create a longing within us to go. For each of us the tug may mean something different. Hurts and disappointments are laid to rest, and good memories become memories and no longer shrines. Whatever the case, God is calling us to move on, to move forward into a new and exciting future. Just like my parents are moving on, so must we embrace the change God has for our lives. Join me as we move on to create new memories.

Not Again!

"The weapons we fight with are not the weapons of the world. On the contrary, they have divine power to demolish strongholds. We demolish arguments and every pretension that sets itself up against the knowledge of God, and we take captive every thought to make it obedient to Christ."
(2 Corinthians 10:4, NIV)

Over the past several months I have been working on clearing away the clutter – in my home, and also in my life. There has been a lot said about eliminating the unnecessary stuff. It felt good to get rid of all the stuff I'd been holding on to; it was nice to be able to walk without tripping. I spent my vacation time this year clearing away stuff in my home. Then, a few days ago, I was in my office when I couldn't put my sketch book anywhere – all available surfaces were heaped with junk. The interesting thing was that it took me under an hour to clean up the mess. Awesome! Before my show-no-mercy housecleaning binge it would have taken me much longer to clean up. Now I have designated "homes" for whatever came in. The same is true of my spiritual life. It was a lot of work to sort through the clutter in my memory. All the garbage that I've found has been astounding! I've dealt with unforgiveness and painful memories, or so I thought. The same feelings came back to haunt me and I wonder how much clearing away and sorting have I really done? Does this sound familiar to you?

I can't help but wonder if the same would be true in our spiritual lives. We've prayed all kinds of prayers and have felt not only relief, but victory. We've dealt with a lot of junk. Yet, the same sorts of things keep coming back with what feels like as much strength as before. We are feeling overwhelmed by the situations we face, feeling the same way, and thinking many of the same thoughts. But what has changed is our ability to wade through the clutter. When we remember the lessons learned, it takes only a short time to wade through the jungle and regain our equilibrium. God has done a deep work in our lives. He has given us the tools with which we combat the enemy of our souls. Now, we must use them.

Oh, to be young, again!

"Be not afraid, O land; be glad and rejoice. Surely the Lord has done great things. Be not afraid, O wild animals, for the open pastures are becoming green. The trees are bearing their fruit; the fig tree and the vine yield their riches. Be glad, O people of Zion, rejoice in the Lord your God, for he has given you a teacher for righteousness. He sends you abundant showers, both autumn and spring rains, as before. The threshing floors will be filled with rain; the vats will overflow with new wine and oil."
(Joel 2:21-24, NIV)

The hills are alive with the sound of music. . . . The Sound of Music, my most favorite movie of all time, opens with a novitiate (student nun) exulting in the wide open spaces of the meadow behind the Abbey. She sings and dances about with abandon that is seldom found in adults. Maria, the star of this musical, continues with a child-like attitude throughout most of the movie. She faces new challenges with courage, but, eventually, runs into a feeling that she cannot deal with. Then she retreats behind a wall of silence and attempts to dig herself deeper into a lifestyle to which she is not called. Her astute Mother Superior knows this and gently pushes her in the direction she has been gifted in.

God wants us to experience joy. He wants us to play with abandon and freedom. Sometimes, however, we become too sophisticated to view the world through the eyes of children. We become hurt, and no longer willing to risk laughter. We can no longer play with abandon because life has become too painful, eliminating any desire to see goodness and light. God gave us all things for us to enjoy, and He is ready to bestow even more on us. The old adage, the more you give, the more you get, applies to the happiness we give to others as we rejoice in all things.

God has given us countless reasons to rejoice and be glad. There are so many ways in which He sends blessings our way. He lavishes His love upon us and gives us gifts. God is eager for us to live life with love and laughter, and enjoy what we have. Let's begin today to live life through the eyes of a child.

The passion play

> "... In the desert prepare the way for the
> Lord; make straight in the wilderness a
> highway for our God. Every valley shall be
> raised up, every mountain and hill made
> low; the rough ground shall become level,
> the rugged places a plain. And the glory of
> the Lord will be revealed, and all mankind
> together will see it. For the mouth of the
> Lord has spoken. "
> (Isaiah 40: 3 & 4, NIV)

Did you know that the Badlands Passion Play has actors in it that aren't even Christians? And did you know that it has been voted the best tourist attraction in Alberta for 2001? Laverne Erickson, founder and director of the Passion Play invited all the pastors in Drumheller to the presentation when he was presenting his dream to the Drumheller Community. At the end of the evening one of the pastors stood up and stated that if it was to be a tourist attraction, why should the churches be involved? One elderly lady answered him, "Why do you suppose God brings 600,000 visitors to our valley every year?"

Miracle after miracle took place as the Badlands Passion Play came into being. Many people would not have heard of the death and resurrection of Jesus Christ had it not been for this incredible tourist attraction. People from the community are involved in every aspect of its production. Truth is being presented in a palatable manner. Laverne Erickson has discovered a way to make the truth acceptable to the viewer. The truth has not been watered down, yet it has been presented to hundreds of people annually.

This is what is happening in Drumheller, Alberta. A man with a vision, a dream, found a way to present the truth. He, and others like him, are making the way plain. The mountains and hills of rules and regulations are being lowered. The truth is being presented. The rough ground of pride and arrogance is becoming level. People are hearing the truth in an unforgettable manner.

I am excited by what I see happening around us. We are seeing many new opportunities to present the truth of God's love. As new opportunities become available to us, let's be quick to become involved. Let's make the way plain for people in our community to come to God.

Real Fruit Trees

"The Christian should resemble a fruit tree, not a Christmas tree. For the gaudy decorations of a Christmas tree are only tied on, whereas fruit grows on a fruit tree."
(John Stott)

My neighbors did a great job of developing their flower bed. Sod was removed and the newly exposed soil was dug up. Topsoil was added and then the resulting fluffy pile was edged with bricks. But they didn't stop there! Rather anxious to see new growth, plastic flowers were "planted". It's quite cute, colorful – and phony! It was pointed out to me that the flowers have even withstood the frosty weather and continue to bloom. They forced the "flowers" to happen. Instead of waiting for real growth to take place, artificial growth was instituted.

That reminded me of how we can be as Christians. We love to see the evidence of God at work. Yet, we become impatient in our passionate pursuit of Him, mistaking our own enthusiasm for the anointing of the Holy Spirit. Activities and programs are implemented simply because it seemed good to us at the moment, and they appear to fit what we'd been praying for. The mistake made is in not waiting for God to speak. Or, perhaps we've just prayed once and felt that was enough.

As Christians, it is imperative to know God's voice. There is no short cut. We must spend time with Him and in His Word so that we know the sound of His voice. It is the only way to become fruit trees, bearing real fruit instead of trees with artificial, gaudy decorations tied on.

On one hand it is much more work to do the latter. We must use our own energy, strength and ingenuity to cause something to appear whereas waiting for God's leading requires none of the above. It necessitates waiting and more waiting and self discipline in reading the Bible and developing our prayer life. When we determine to become genuine fruit trees bearing luscious fruit, we must learn to let go of our dreams, aspirations and ambitions. God will cause us to bear fruit that brings Him honor and glory. He gave us his Word on that!

> *"You did not choose me, but I chose you and appointed you to go and bear fruit—fruit that will last. . ."*
>
> *(John 15:16a, NIV)*

M. JOYCE HALVORSON

A
POTPURRI
OF
INSPIRATION

Answering Machines

"Call to me and I will answer you and tell you great and unsearchable things you do not know."
(Jeremiah 33:3, NIV)

No one likes talking to a machine. But most of us do it. Very few people do not have an answering machine or voice mail. When the line is busy or the person we wish to speak to is not home we are requested to leave a message and someone will get right back to us. Maybe calls are being monitored and that person only wants to talk to certain people. They could be sleeping and turned the ringers off -- I've done that. There is any number of reasons for having an answering machine. In our fast paced society it seems that we cannot wait for a call to be returned. Sometimes, we leave messages that are not received and our calls are not returned.

My phone seldom rings, probably because no one knows what

shift I am working. I like to take calls from my friends, but I am not always available so they leave messages which I return (most of the time). I have several extra features on my phone. But it seems that there is always one more feature that my phone provider wants me to subscribe to.

My husband used to sing about a "telephone to glory". The song went on about the direct line we had to the Father. The line was never busy; we always had direct, instant access whenever we called. That song was an old one. But it spoke volumes about how easy it is to talk to God -- about anything at all. He is never so busy talking to someone else that He doesn't have time for us. God doesn't have an answering machine, neither does he have voice mail, call waiting or call forwarding. He doesn't have a conference call feature on his phone. Whenever we call, he answers -- right away. We have instant access. He doesn't monitor his calls like some of us do. He is not so busy helping someone else that He will not talk to us. What is even better is that he is WAITING to hear from us.

Since the "telephone to glory" is so easy to use, isn't it a wonder that more people aren't using it? One phone call. That's all it takes, and we have all of heaven ready to help us. Let's get that phone line busy with our calls. Let's begin today!

Call display

".. . whatever is true, whatever is noble,
whatever is right . . . if anything is excellent
or praiseworthy--think about such things . .
. and the God of peace will be with you."
(Philippians 4:8-9, NIV)

I just purchased a new phone. My old one was working part time
-- probably because I dropped it too many times. This one is capable of several functions, some of which I've programmed it to
do, other features I have not subscribed to. For the first time I have
call display. That way, I can screen my calls. If it is someone I really
don't want to talk to, I just don't answer it, and the call automati-
cally goes to my voice mail. Sometimes I am already on the phone
when I hear a beeping noise. This means that I have another call
coming in. Usually I choose to ignore the second call. Even though
the second caller may not leave a message on my voice mail, I can
determine who called by the click of a button.

We have messages coming into our minds and our spirits continually. Some of these messages are from God and some of them are from Satan. We can be having a great time with God, when we begin to hear a beeping in our ear. It's another message demanding attention. We can tell at a glance who is calling and choose to ignore it. That's what we do whenever we say no to Satan and yes to God. Life is a series of choices, some of them hard to make. But each time we look, and quickly decide to ignore wrong messages, we are choosing to obey God.

Some calls are hard to ignore while others are important. We can carry on conversations while waiting for other calls to come in. We can also tell if we are receiving any nuisance calls and ignore them. When we choose to listen to wrong thoughts, our lives will be one interruption after another. But when we choose to ignore the nuisance calls Satan sends our way, we will be rewarded with God's peace and presence.

I am enjoying the call display feature on my phone. I know who is calling and can begin to formulate an answer. I enjoy my spiritual call display even more because it lets me know who is calling.

Have you activated your call display?

Call forwarding

"For God did not give us a spirit of timidity,
but a spirit of power, of love and of
self-discipline."
(2 Timothy 1:7, NIV)

"Neither do I condemn you."
(John 8:11, NKJV)

A couple of weeks ago I was expecting an important call. But I couldn't wait. Another appointment was impending. All was well, however, because Telus, my phone provider, had talked me into purchasing a bundle, or package, and one of the features included was call forwarding. My house phone went on call forwarding and away I went. The cell phone rang several times that day in a variety of places. Some of the situations proved to be quite hilarious, yet I was able to go about my business and receive calls.

We are like that sometimes. We put our lives on call forwarding. We get so busy living our lives that we don't take the time to wait. In our hectic lifestyle, we are out and about, frantically hoping not to miss anything important. At other times we are at home but we just want someone else to deal with the calls. Maybe we just needed to rest, or the calls may have been harassing in nature. I've talked about call display, which enables us to screen our calls. When this feature is combined with call forwarding, we are able to screen our calls and then, by a click of a button, forward that call without answering it. I especially like that concept when it comes to my walk with God.

When a call comes in, I can observe who it is from and decide whether or not to answer it. Then, in an instant, call forward it to God's phone line. When the thoughts coming into my head are condemning in nature, or fearful, I know they are not from God. By sending that suggestion to God, I am committing it to the finished work on the cross. The blood of Jesus has paid for my sin. The past has been wiped clean.

Just like the call display and call forwarding features on my phone, our spiritual lives are affected by how we choose to direct the thoughts and suggestions coming into our minds. It's a choice we must make minute by minute. We can choose to activate those features or we can deal with everything in our own strength. The choice is ours. Activate your call display/call forwarding today.

God of the silence

*"The Lord is my shepherd, I shall lack
nothing. He makes me lie down in green
pastures, he leads me beside quiet waters."*
(Psalm 23: 1&2, NIV)

While I was thinking about this, I saw two pictures. The first was
that of a waterfall. The sound of the roaring water as it tumbled
over the precipice was incredible. It was an awesome sound, and
almost deafening in its intensity! Not another sound could be
heard. One would have needed a megaphone to speak to the person standing right next to him. Songs describing God's majesty
came to my mind as I pondered this picture: God was God of the
waterfalls!

The scene changed. This time the scene was of a quiet park-like
setting. There was a river nearby with people resting near its edge.
They were convalescing. They'd been wounded and hurt. Now
they needed some rest. It was peaceful, and not a ripple could be
found on the water. The temperature was just right: not too hot

and not too cold. It was easy to understand that God had made this setting as well.

Just like these two pictures portray a loving God who wants nothing more than to bless his children, so do our services portray the same loving God longing to give us the very best He has. Sometimes He noisily lavishes His love upon us, and other times he bids us rest. Some church services are awesome pictures of a mighty God, living, and moving, among His people. He is pouring out His Spirit among us in a new, fresh way. We are not able to predict how and when God will move. We only know that He is moving.

It is easy to recognize God at work when we see the dancing and hear the weeping and shouting. But it is difficult, for some of us, to understand that God is still at work in the silence, and in those quiet moments when no one is uttering a word or an instrument is being played. The silence is almost deafening. We are alone with our own thoughts, and may feel threatened by our lack of words directed towards God, but God is not. In these silent times his still, small, gentle voice can be heard. In the silence He is at work on the inner man, accomplishing what only God can do. God is God of the silence!

Distractions

"But those who hope in the Lord will renew
their strength. They will soar on wings like
eagles; they will run and not grow weary,
they will walk and not be faint."
(Isaiah 40:31, NIV)

Part of my job includes answering the phones while completing multiple other tasks; most of the time I stop what I am doing and answer the phone. Other times I may be in the middle of doing something when 6 other tasks come to mind. If I am not disciplined in my work habits I would easily be running around in circles doing busy things but not accomplishing anything.

When we set aside time to pray, counsel others, write a note of encouragement, or write a bulletin article, all kinds of distractions are found. The dog barks and the phone rings. Oh, oh, there's the door bell. Dust suddenly becomes an inch thick, daring us to do something about it. Our minds know that if we become heavily involved in serving, it will lose its place of authority in our life.

If we persist, they will become completely replaced by Christ's mind. Our minds will then think Christ's thoughts and our pens will write God's words.

Whatever will serve to take our minds and our hearts away from doing what God has called us to do is what Satan will do. He intends to win the war. However, we are not among his troupes. We must fight to maintain control. Fighting, not in the sense of arguing or using all our energy rebuking the devil, but rather, in praying and asking God to come and take control, and then simply getting on with the job at hand. It's much like a toddler learning to walk. He stands and moves forward. He falls and gets up and moves forward again. The frustration is in the time it takes. Learning to recognize the distractions and smoke screens the enemy sends our way takes practice and concentrated effort. It is a spiritual skill that is developed.

Father, help us to keep our focus on you. May we develop a mind set that continually hears your voice. We do not want to become weary from trying because it is with your strength that we succeed and not our own. We long to soar like the eagles and not cower like their prey. Help us to walk in your ways so the distractions of life will not sap our vitality and cause us to become tired. Teach us to wait on you.

The rhythm of the music

"But Joshua had commanded the people,
'Do not give a war cry, do not raise your
voices, do not say a word until the day I tell
you to shout. Then shout!"
(Joshua 6; 10, NIV)

My deep water running instructor loves music with a definite beat. She knows that if we will only be quiet and listen to the beat, we will be able to successfully complete the various exercises. Well, an easier time, at least. Occasionally, I will chat to another participant instead; and it's as though I lose all my hearing! Do I have to work harder to catch up: Oh, no. I simply calm myself and listen to the music, allowing my body to feel the rhythm. I can't gain what has already been lost, but I can improve on the remainder of the class.

We Christians are just like the deep water running participants.

We get in the pool where all the action is happening. We are so excited to be there that we engage in conversations with fellow Christians, and forget our purpose for being. We recount all that God has done in our lives and give Him praise. It's exciting living in a Holy Spirit charged atmosphere! But then we forget our purpose for being and wonder why, in all the excitement, has nothing been accomplished.

The Israelites were outside Jericho. They'd seen God do some amazing things through them. They hadn't always been obedient; but they'd been forgiven and they moved on. It must have been hard to be absolutely quiet in the face of the enemy. Yet, that's what God had commanded. There was no whispering, only the trumpets made any noise. They waited; they were quiet; they were obedient. When the command was given they shouted and walls were destroyed in an instant.

The armies of Israel had learned the rhythm of God's music, and they marched in time to the beat. God wants us to be just like that. There are so many amazing things that will take place when we learn the rhythm of God's music. When we march in time to the beat, the yoke will become easy, the burden light. There is still hard work to be done, but it will all be accomplished because we've become silent, listened to the music and learned to move in time to the beat.

The road not yet traveled

When I was a young girl, we had autograph books in which short messages or poems such as the one above were collected. The above was my mother's favorite whenever she was asked for yet another autograph. That little poem still holds a challenge for me. My future is uncharted: I can choose to take a pathway that others have taken, or I can choose to follow my dreams, wherever they may lead.

The well traveled pathway has been worn smooth by its frequent use. It's a popular path, easier going with no challenges. It's a simple matter to fit in with the trendy crowd.

The other pathway, the one less traveled is the one that holds terror for any one contemplating its use. There are no markers along the way, and the pitfalls have yet to be discovered. It's a lonely road, for many times the obstacles we will face will be the objections of those who are close to us. The untraveled byways beckon us. We understand that there may be danger along the way, but with preparation behind us, we boldly set out. It is more than a road less traveled; it is a way never traversed by anyone.

Many challenges are ahead; and we have two choices. We can choose to follow the voice of God or we can choose to go our own way. God's way may seem to be the well worn path, yet it is not. It is, in fact, the road yet to be charted.

When our lives come to an end may we be able to turn around, look back, and say with Louisa May Alcott,

> "Life is my college. May I graduate well, and earn some honors!"

> *(Louisa May Alcott)*

When we see Jesus may we all hear,

> ".... *Well done, thou good and faithful servant: thou hast been faithful over a few things, I will make thee ruler over many things: enter thou into the joy of thy Lord."*

> *(Matthew 25:21, KJV)*

God has a plan for each one of us; a plan that we will not discover until we set out on the road not yet traveled.

M. JOYCE HALVORSON

Medication - Take as needed

*"Come unto me, all you who are weary and
burdened, and I will give you rest, Take my
yoke upon you and learn from me, for I am
gentle and humble in heart, and you will
find rest for your souls. For my yoke is easy
and my burden is light."*
(*Matthew* 11: 28-30, *NIV*)

No one really enjoys taking pills. Physicians order appropriate
medication according to strict guidelines. They may order a pain
medication to be taken on a regular basis; a prn, or as needed, dose
will also be ordered for those times when the regular dose is ineffective. This is because there is no way of knowing exactly how
much pain and discomfort a patient is able to tolerate. (As a side
note, an injury will not heal as quickly if the patient is experiencing a lot of pain.) I was thinking about this when the comparison
to our walk with the Lord came to my mind.

We are to regularly read the Bible for the simple reason of reading God's love letter to us. It could easily be compared to taking our vitamins. There is no immediate effect felt. However, over time, one can begin to feel the effects of taking these supplements. They are good for us, and we will reap the benefits eventually. The same is true of reading and studying God's Word. We do not always receive a "wow moment" when reading it. However, with time we gain wisdom and direction from its pages because we've absorbed the intended principles and have incorporated them into our lives.

Repeatedly we find ourselves running to God and His Word, looking for answers to the stressors of life. Jesus urges us to turn to Him whenever the weariness of life becomes too heavy for us. His yoke is easy, He says, and His burden is not too hard for us to handle. Just like a "take as needed" pain medication cannot help us unless we swallow it, so we cannot reap the benefits of God's way unless we pick up the Bible and read it. We must ingest it for any benefit to be felt. When we consume God's Word on a regular basis, and devour some more when life is tougher than normal, we will reap an amazing benefit. Devouring God's Word starts with the first bite. Let's begin today.

M. JOYCE HALVORSON

Shades of grey

"... God is light; in him there is no darkness
at all. ... if we walk in the light, as he is
in the light, we have fellowship with one
another, and the blood of Jesus, his Son,
purifies us from all sin."
(1 John 1:5 & 7, NIV)

An invaluable lesson was learned when I started sketching. I am a very black and white person, and tend to see situations as either one way or another. But when a local artist and friend, volunteered to teach me how to sketch, I found that things just weren't all that easy. In sketching, it is the varying shades of the pencil that create the picture. I had to decide where the light was coming from. This was so that I could shade the parts of the picture hidden from the light source darker. Sometimes the shading became almost black while other parts of my picture were left untouched by my pencil. What made the difference was the source of light, and all that it touched.

We will BE in the light as we turn to God. Our faces will be warmed by His presence. All darkness will be gone as we face the light, and as we acknowledge the truth of God's Word. We will continue in darkness and stumble around blindly only until Light is allowed into our lives.

God is light. He is not limited to being merely a "source of light", but is complete light. There are no shadows when God is present, neither is there any artificial light. The closer we move towards God and all His brilliance, the more light will shine all around us. Nothing can be hidden from God as He illuminates every area of our being.

We must walk in this light, completing each step that is mapped out for us; there will be more work for us to do in ridding ourselves of filth and decay, commonly known as sin. There are others on the same journey as we are – walking in the light. It is with these very people that we will have fellowship because we've learned our lessons and been obedient to God. The good news is that there are no shades of gray in God's presence because there are no shadows. He is everywhere, continually illuminating our lives with His presence.

Talk to me, God!

"The heavens declare the glory of God; the skies proclaim the work of his hands. Day after day they pour forth speech ..."
(Psalm 19:1, 2, NIV)

One of the moms at our Wednesday morning Bible Study was telling us how they'd instituted quiet times for their children. These quiet times were simply age appropriate lengths of time set aside for each of the children to be quiet and listen for God's voice to speak to them. And He did speak! God does speak to each of us. He speaks to us in countless ways; His Word, through people (both Christians and unsaved), and through nature itself.

We have all heard that in order to know someone, we must spend time with them. If a friend were to send a letter, we would take time to read it. In the same way, God has sent us a letter – the Bible. We get to know Him as we read what He has written. It is our owner's manual and guidebook for daily living. There are examples within its pages that help us understand how God works and all He wants to do in our lives. If we fail to read, we fail to hear.

Over the years God has used people to encourage me and to point me in the way I needed to go. Both Christians and non-Christians have spoken truth into my life. Those words have encouraged me and issued a challenge. It was God that spoke to me through those people. Had I not been quiet and listened to their voices, I would not have heard.

God hung the sun, moon, and stars in place, and now one look at them declares the magnificence of our Creator. When we fail to look around us at the works of God's hands we fail to hear God speak.

Yes, God speaks to us. It is our responsibility and choice whether we hear. We must be careful to not put God in a box and expect Him to speak in any one particular way. The youngster was quiet and expected to hear God speak, and so we must do the same. Whatever way God speaks, we must be prepared to be silent and say as Samuel said,

"Speak, for your servant is listening. . ."

(I Samuel 3:10, NIV)

Are you listening?

The counselor

*"But the counsellor, the Holy Spirit, whom
the Father will send in my name, will
teach you all things and will remind you of
everything I have said to you."*
(John 14:26, NIV)

Jesus taught his disciples continually. There was never a break in what He did and said. If they were walking on the road, He was busy teaching. If He was talking with people, He was their example of how they should conduct themselves. Just before He was crucified Jesus told them about the Holy Spirit whose primary function was to come along side of them and remind them Jesus' teaching. The same function exists today.

As we study the Word of God and apply it to our daily lives, the Holy Spirit will assist us and remind us of those things we need to remember. We will not know everything all the time. Rather, we will remember those things we need to know at the time we need them. It's mind boggling! Whenever we need wisdom, peace, or the right word, He will be there. It all starts with the Bible. We must be studying, reading and meditating on it. If we have never read its pages, we cannot be reminded of what we've read. As we read and meditate on something, it becomes a part of us. The Holy Spirit has been sent to us to remind us of those things.

Too often, we have relegated the Holy Spirit to something weird and wonderful. We've been taught that the Holy Spirit is for church, and speaking in tongues is for those moments when we need a special word from God. The Holy Spirit is for those times, and He is also for our daily lives. The Holy Spirit is involved in our daily lives. Do we need wisdom in raising our children? The Holy Spirit is there with us. Do we need wisdom in relating to our spouse? The Holy Spirit is with us. What about our friendships? The Holy Spirit is with us.

You are welcome, Holy Spirit, in our lives. Continue reminding us of the path we must walk. Help us remember all those things we have been taught from the Bible. We invite you into our lives; we choose to listen to your voice today. You are welcome; you are needed in this place.

M. JOYCE HALVORSON

That's not fair!

"To do justice and judgment is more
acceptable to the Lord than sacrifice."
(Proverbs 21:3, NIV)

We've been wronged! We say that we've forgiven, but all we've done is bury the offence. At a later time we uncover the hurt, and our internal dialogue begins. We know exactly what we would say to them when we meet them again. We'd give them a piece of our mind! On the other hand, during those quiet times when we are just contemplating life, is our internal dialogue entirely fair? It may not matter, we argue. Who is going to be hurt by what we think? Yet, this is exactly what Philippians 4:8 is saying to us. We are to think on, or meditate on those things that are fair or just.

According to some commentaries this would mean that our thoughts are agreeable to the rules of justice in all our dealings – minus the contamination that comes from sin. Sometimes we tend to embellish a story, making our involvement favorable or minimal – depending upon the circumstance. Either way, we are attempting to make ourselves sound good in the ears of the hearer. Then we attempt to assuage our guilt by becoming generous in our actions. Again we argue, "No harm done."

I beg to differ. When our thought life is largely dominated by exaggerated internal dialogue, we are in fact, harming ourselves. At some juncture we will also be harming others because we will react out of our incorrect, sinful dialogue. We may even wonder where the reaction came from, thinking it was entirely out of character for us to think that way. I have had the unpleasant experience of exactly this occurring in my life. It has only been recently that I recognized it for what it was and took it to God in repentance. Has the incorrect internal dialogue stopped? No, because my old sinful human nature does not want to die. I have been learning that each time I repent of my unjust thoughts the old human nature has been dealt another death blow.

Father, help us to be more like you in our thoughts. Shine the search light of your Holy Spirit into all areas of our lives so that we might rid ourselves of impurities.

M. JOYCE HALVORSON

That's offensive!

"Finally, be strong in the Lord and in his mighty power. Put on the full armor of God so that you can take your stand against the devil's schemes."
(Ephesians 6:10, 11, NIV)

I know we've all heard it said that the armor of God found in Ephesians is only good as long as we face the enemy. There is nothing to protect our backsides; but not only do we need to face the enemy; we must also go towards those things that are threatening to annihilate us. However, what most of us have failed to realize is what our football pundits all know, "the best defensive is a good offense". The players do not sit around and wait for the opposing team to come to them. Rather, they are continually on the attack, looking for ways to score a goal and to wear the enemy down. The same is true of us as Christians. We do not sit around in our pews on Sundays and in our chairs at home and wait for things to happen.

We get up, put on our armor and get busy. Advancing the kingdom of God is what we are all called to do. It means living out our daily lives in such a way that brings honor to God. Simply put, when we are truly living in the power of the Holy Spirit and are allowing Him to flow through us, we will be attracting people to Christ.

It also means going beyond what we have done before and leave the familiar. God wants us to do something that we have never done before or never thought we were capable of doing.

> See, I am doing a new thing! Now it springs up; do you not perceive it? I am making a way in the desert and streams in the wasteland."

> (Isaiah 43:19, NIV)

God will not be put in a box. He wants to fill the voids in our lives and communities that have been vacant, and He needs us to be His spokesperson and his conduit. We may be intimidated by the need, but with His help, we can do all things because He gives us the strength to do so. So let's just get up and do it! We are, after all, offensive people!

There's more!

> "Therefore, if any man be in Christ, he is a
> new creature: old things are passed away;
> behold, all things are become new."
> (2 Corinthians 5:17, KJV)

I have an awesome poster! The picture is of a statue, probably of gold or bronze. Part of this gold has been peeled away to reveal a beautiful diamond. The old layers hang loosely around the waist. The man (statue) appears to be in a great deal of pain. He looks as though he is trying to push the pain away with one hand above the other.

The statue was already beautiful to look at. It was of great value. But the owner knew there was more, that beneath the glistening exterior lay a treasure of infinitely greater value. So he began the process of pealing away the beauty. At first it looked like a tragedy had occurred. The once beautiful surfaces were now marred. The statue was useless. It began experiencing pain and objected violently to the process! The owner, a master craftsman, kept working on it. Over time a new object appeared. The once hidden treasure was revealed for everyone to enjoy.

We, as Christians, are just like that statue. We are already precious to God. We've been bought with a price, and are loved by our master. But there's more! Underneath the gold there is a treasure of far greater value. The stripping, cleansing process begins when we give the Holy Spirit permission to work in our lives. Often we become impatient with the process, longing for completion. But God has another plan. He slows the process down when we are in need of rest. At other times the process is sped up and we feel out of control. The good news is that God knows just how much we can bear at any one time. He sees us as we are. He knows that underneath the entire facade lies a diamond, a precious gem.

It is with immense care that the layers are pealed away. Just as the master craftsman takes care to gently remove crusty layers slowly and carefully, God will gently remove the old crusty layers and reveal the hidden treasure within. The process is often painful, but we can be assured that God will complete the work begun in us--in His time.

Snow

"......though your sins are like scarlet, they
shall be as white as snow..."
(Isaiah 1:18, NIV)

I love the snow. It is simply amazing the way everything is blanketed in white, shining, sparkling white. When one of my boys was a toddler he looked out one morning and was delighted by the snow that had fallen during the night. "I'ceam, mommy, I'ceam!" he shouted. He thought there was ice cream all over the ground and he wanted some!

The Israelites had been protected. God helped them conquer their enemies. They were a strong nation, but God was not pleased with them; they had gone their own way. They knew what God wanted, but chose a different way. They were a rebellious people, and they were losing what had been given to them. Into this setting came the Word of the Lord. God had had enough of their rebellion! Yet, He was willing to forgive them and cause them to become a prize jewel, sparkling in the light. They would be even more amazing than freshly fallen snow.

As snow falls, it traps pollutants, thus causing the snow to be impure. It still sparkles in the bright sunlight, but it is impure. There are many toxins within it. God was saying that He would make them whiter than snow. There would be absolutely no impurities, and no imperfections. There is no indication how long this would take, however. All He required was a change of heart.

We are like those people of long ago. We have become set in our ways and refuse to let go of sin; the impurities in our lives. We have been hurt by others and tenaciously cling to the pain of unforgiveness. We have chosen to go our own way, choosing rather to sort things out ourselves. All the while God is waiting. He is looking for a change of heart; and then He will begin the cleansing process. He has not given us any indication of how long this process will take. All He has said is that even though we have done the most horrible thing imaginable, He will forgive us and make us clean and new. He has given us His Word on this, and He will not go back on it. The process will begin as we learn to trust Him to remove the impurities, causing us to sparkle in the light of His Son.

Smile at the storm

*"He got up, rebuked the wind and said to
the waves, 'Quiet! Be still!' Then the wind
died down and it was completely calm."*
(*Mark 4:39, NIV*)

Do you feel as though you've been hammered straight into the ground? It seems like life has a way of piling up on top of us until we cannot see which way to go! Over the past few weeks I've commented to friends and co-workers that it sure would be nice if we could deal with one thing at a time. Unfortunately, it's never that easy. Life tends to be like the weather around here. First, unseasonably warm temperatures, followed by a sudden drop to the deep freeze! Don't forget the snow, rain and Chinook winds that could easily occur in the same day!

I was at a Bible Study when the leader asked each of us to use weather conditions to describe our lives that day. Words such as turbulent, calm, sunny, and windy were used. That particular day someone said that they felt as though they were in a fog; they weren't worried because the Son was shining down on them and would soon burn the fog away.

That came to my mind as I was contemplating my life over the past few weeks. It's been turbulent, and there have been storms. I felt gale force winds blowing. In the midst of all this, a chorus started floating through my mind. I have nothing to fear! Christ is in my vessel. He is, in fact, the Captain of my ship and is at the helm. It doesn't matter how high the waves become or how hard the wind blows.

Jesus and his disciples were in a storm. He was so calm and comfortable that He fell asleep while the storm raged! The disciples were terrified and woke Jesus with impassioned questions of whether He cared!

He was the Master of the boat then and He is still the Master of the winds and the rain today. He is more than willing to come into our lives, calm the turbulence, and give us courage to face whatever storms we may encounter.

Supreme stubborness

> "You too, be patient and stand firm,"
> (James 5:8, NIV)

I haven't heard very many positive comments about basic training for a new recruit to the armed forces. What I have heard indicates that it is a punishing and arduous time period, grueling work that takes a great deal of self discipline to complete. Once this training period is finished, the person then becomes a full fledged soldier. Combined with basic training, ongoing training exercises equip him to prepare for combat. The same is true of us as Christians.

We are in a war. We've all had basic training through Sunday School, Bible Studies and sermons. Yet, the real war begins once we leave the safe haven of the church building or the gathering place for small groups. Once a person has renounced and torn down a stronghold (an incorrect thought pattern or habit) in hisorher life, the war has only just begun. Satan will not take lightly any defeat. He will not leave without a fierce struggle for reinstatement. He likes the influence he's had in our thoughts, and we must be prepared for war.

> "Now when an unclean spirit goes out of a man, it passes through waterless places, seeking rest, and does not find it. Then it says, 'I will return to my house from which I came'"

> (Matthew 12:43-44)

Once we have repented of our sin, we can anticipate the devil wanting to come back. While the victory has been won when we renounced Satan's hold on our lives, we must, of necessity, continue to stand firm, refusing to give any ground back to the enemy. Should the struggle continue for some time, it may be necessary to examine our lives once again for any other impediments to our growth. Again, we stand firm. We must continually, and consistently, say no to the devil. It is a war we are in, and as long as we remain firmly committed to Christ and obedient to Him, we will win.

This struggle is only a temporary one. It will end.

> "... the testing of your faith develops perseverance. Perseverance must finish its work so that you may be mature and complete, not lacking anything."

> (James 1:3-4, NIV)

Never give up! God is faithful and will complete the work He has begun. Our persistence will produce the desired end -- if we stand firm.

M. JOYCE HALVORSON

The upward journey

"For since the creation of the world God's invisible qualities—his eternal power and divine nature—have been clearly seen, being understood from what has been made, so that men are without excuse. For although they knew God, they neither glorified him as God nor gave thanks to him, but their thinking became futile and their foolish hearts were darkened."
(Romans 1:20-21, NIV)

It is of utmost importance that we learn to tear down or destroy any foolish or incorrect imaginations. So often incorrect thinking gets us into trouble, and it all begins with failing to glorify God. It is when we recognize the truth that we can begin to change.

The people Paul was talking about in this verse had knowledge of God. Yet, they failed to recognize Him in anything they did. They were vain in their thinking and gave themselves credit for everything good that happened. This being the case, they probably managed to blame someone else for anything that went wrong. These same people never thanked God for anything either. Next, in the downward spiral, their thinking became useless and of no value.

So often we are just like those people. We work hard at what we do and take all the credit for it, failing to acknowledge God's hand in what we've done. When someone compliments us, it's ok to say thank you and accept the praise. However, it would be even more acceptable to refer our success to God, either at that moment or at a later time. Many times, we fail to do this and, unwittingly, have begun the downward spiral. We become preoccupied with thoughts that are of no value and therefore, of no importance. We've begun to develop a rut out of which we cannot climb. After allowing these inconsequential thoughts to persist, our hearts become darkened. Our lives have become so cluttered with trivial matters there is no longer sufficient room for light to appear.

There is hope, even yet. The most effective way to begin the upward journey is by repenting and asking God to forgive us for failing to recognize Him at work in our lives. The journey we've begun has many lessons for us to learn. But as we persist,

> *"We demolish arguments and every pretension that sets itself up against the knowledge of God, and we take captive every thought to make it obedient to Christ."*

> *(2 Corinthians 10:5, NIV)*

     M. JOYCE HALVORSON

You are what you eat

*"Do you not know that your body is a
temple of the Holy Spirit, who is in you,
whom you have received from God? You are
not your own; you were bought at a price.
Therefore honor God with your body."
(I Corinthians 6:19-20, NIV)*

I haven't been feeling very well the last few days. My energy level is low and life has become gray and dull. It is true that living a balanced life is a continual challenge. But, with God's help, I've managed to do what I've found in front of me to do. God has been especially close to me and I've recognized what He has been doing in my life. I see some major changes taking place, and I am delighted. The only thing that's really changed at all is the food I eat. The past several days have found me consuming more junk food than normal.

It was comforting during the storm last weekend to eat sweets, even though I knew unhealthy food affected my emotions. Sugar is rapidly digested and then my energy level drops because I've literally run out of fuel, whereas healthy food takes longer to digest, giving me a steady source of energy.

Then there is the junk food my mind likes to eat – inappropriate books, unwholesome TV shows. Since we are triune beings consisting of body, soul, and spirit, it is quite reasonable to anticipate a slump in energy when my spirit and soul have not been nurtured, or whenever my diet has not been balanced with healthy food.

Sometimes we pay too much attention to one aspect of our lives and not enough to another. We tend to focus on our spirits and neglect our bodies, or vice versa. We must care for our spirits by reading wholesome books and disciplining our minds to accept those thoughts that are pure. We must also nurture our bodies with healthy eating. When any one part of our being is neglected the rest of us will suffer.

When life loses its sparkle, let's take a look at what we have been feeding ourselves. Have we been dishonoring God by not eating what is best for us? Let's begin today to take care of our bodies so that God will be honored in all that we do.

M. JOYCE HALVORSON

Vaccinations

"The trouble with some of us is that we have been inoculated with small doses of Christianity which keep us from catching the real thing."
(Author unknown)

When my boys were babies, they received all the usual vaccinations, most of which were "live" minute doses of the actual disease. This was supposed to help their bodies develop antibodies that would, in turn, ward off the disease. These small doses prevented them from either catching the real thing or from contracting a severe case of that disease. Now, most vaccinations are synthetic, but the principle remains the same. One small injection is meant to keep us from getting the real live full blown case of a disease.

The same is true for us as Christians. We have been "serving the Lord for a while" and have become dissatisfied with ourselves. What has happened is that we've stagnated in our growth as Christians. Without the continual flow of the Holy Spirit in us and through us we have become stagnant pools with no outlet. We have allowed what was originally a live case of Christianity to become a vaccination. What was once the beginning of a truly incredible journey has become the final destination. We cannot move on because our experience has dictated otherwise. But God is a fluid God; He is constantly on the move, and there is always something fresh and new to experience.

We have received the Word as it was presented to us, and assumed that we'd received the whole truth. If anything didn't line up with our personal doctrine, it was rejected as being untrue because it didn't fit the parameters already established. Sadly, we'd been inoculated and are unable to receive the real thing. That's ok when we think of all the disease in the world. But I would rather have the real thing when it comes to Christianity.

Some vaccinations must be repeated – their effect diminishes with time. I am certainly hoping and praying that all the artificiality will be gone from my life. I want to be real. The imitation vaccination will eventually lose its potency as I choose to allow the Holy Spirit to work in my life. We do not need a vaccination; we need the real thing! Join me in a grand infusion of the Holy Spirit in our lives.

M. JOYCE HALVORSON

Virtuous thinking

". . . if there be any virtue. . . think on these
things."
(Philippians 4:8, NIV)

I like making lists, grocery lists, to do lists, etc. As each item is completed, it is crossed off. In that way I know when something is done. I find this most effective when I am faced with a new procedure at work, or I have a lot of things to do. Making a list when I feel pressured de-stresses my life immeasurably.

Our minds are constantly bombarded with inappropriate thoughts and suggestions. Television, magazines, and newspapers all produce massive quantities of bad news, thoughts and ideas that weigh our minds down. Time spent mulling over negative aspects of life, or time spent considering impure ideas, can corrupt our thoughts and eventually our actions. A thought just passing through cannot do any harm. But something we think about or fantasize about becomes ingrained in our memories and may eventually portray itself, incorrectly, as truth.

"For as he thinketh in his heart, so is he. . ."

(Proverbs 23:7, KJV)

It is so important to think true thoughts. Paul sums this subject up when he says that if there is anything wholesome, we should think about it, or meditate on it. Conversely, if we are dwelling on inappropriate thoughts, pictures, T.V. shows, books, etc, then we will eventually become like them. None of us choose to become immoral people; there is a path that is taken to arrive at such a place. In our verse for today, Paul is advising us to think wholesome thoughts.

He has given us another item in our check list for improving our mental and emotional health. As we spend time in God's Word we begin to understand His plan and purpose for our lives. The Bible contains many instructions for how we are to live and examples of those who lived godly lives as well as those who failed.

We must assess our thought life and what influences it. Then we must make the necessary changes in what we allow a resting place in our minds. Let's begin to day to meditate on wholesome things. We will have the pleasure of watching our mental and emotional health improve.

What an attitude!

"Your attitude should be the same as that
of Christ Jesus..."
(Philippians 2: 5, NIV)

She's got an attitude! Whenever we hear that phrase, we immediately think of anything inappropriate or negative. This person may think more highly of himself than he ought to think. Sometimes people have the mistaken idea that the world owes them something and that they do not have any responsibility in a difficult situation. It is almost always someone else's fault or problem. These are difficult people to deal with. In the workplace they disrupt the otherwise smooth running of a business and generally make life miserable for almost any co-worker. Attitudes are a part of every day life. They are what shape our actions. Attitudes define who we are and how well we do what we do. They can be defined as a mind set, or a definite way of thinking, or a strong will.

Jesus had an attitude! The above scripture tells us that He knew who He was. The son of God did not abuse His position of authority. He could have called thousands of angels to rescue him but He did not. He knew who He was. He was secure in his position. He became a servant and humbled himself. Obedience to God's plan was the focal point of his life. Jesus knew what lay ahead for him and agonized over it but he remained obedient. From a human perspective, it appeared that everything was lost because of it. This was not the case, and eventually, the sacrifice Jesus made became the foundation of all we know today.

We are instructed to have the same attitude. We must first become secure in who we are in God. We can enjoy close fellowship with God because of Jesus' obedience. Next, we must develop the heart attitude of a servant, considering others of more importance than ourselves, constantly looking for ways to help each other. Finally, we are to show our care and concern. Never are we to conduct ourselves as though we are superior to anyone. God has saved us and redeemed us. We are to conduct our lives in such a way as to bring glory and not dishonor to the name of Christ.

Loving, serving, giving – what an attitude! Let's begin today to develop the attitude of Christ.

What an attitude – Part 2

> "No servant can serve two masters. Either he will hate the one and love the other, or he will be devoted to the one and despise the other."
>
> (Luke 16:13, NIV)

We say someone has a bad attitude when they refuse to accept correction. Bad attitudes persist when a driver cuts someone off, thinking that they have the right to be ahead. We can also be guilty of having a bad attitude when we refuse to accept who we are in Christ, wishing we could say something other than who we are. Jesus had an attitude of a servant while he was here on earth and it is this attitude we are to develop when we wish to have the mind of Christ.

A servant readily submits to the authority over him He may not agree with what he's been asked to do but a servant will follow the instructions without question. A true servant is also faithful to his master. He does not divulge confidential information nor does he criticize his master. This servant is completely trustworthy and his master has confidence in him. This same servant also knows that he is accountable to his master and only him. What anyone else says is of no consequence.

".. ... To his own master he stands or falls. .."

(Romans 14:4)

Each hospital unit has a manager. Each of these managers has a particular way they like to see things done. My manager likes things a certain way and I do it that way. Although I may have said what I think and whether I agree with their decision or not, but still I do things their way. It simply doesn't matter at all if another manager doesn't agree with my work. The same is true of us spiritually. We are only accountable to God and to those he has placed in authority over us.

How do we develop the attitude of a servant? It all begins when we make a decision to follow Jesus and continues as we spend time in prayer and in reading the Bible. Eventually, it becomes second nature to us. We will not have to think about what we are to do. We will just know what our instructions are as we seek to serve.

Jesus had an attitude – of a servant. Do you?

Where did that come from?

"May the words of my mouth and the meditation of my heart be pleasing in your sight, O Lord,"
(Psalm 19:14, NIV)

The human mind is fascinating. We can have thoughts, ideas, and feelings that we are aware of. We can also have other thoughts, ideas and feelings in our minds that we are not aware of. When I came across this concept, I began thinking about how this could affect our behavior. If we feast our eyes on things that are not good for us, it could eventually work its way into our spirits and minds in such a way that we are influenced by them. In much the same way we can also be influenced by what we hear being said. Even though it may be meant as a joke, our spirits can receive a belittling remark which could affect the way we view ourselves and others.

We do not always remember what is within our hearts. If we allow bitter thoughts to take root in our hearts and minds, then we should not be surprised when anger and resentment form our conversations and conscious thoughts. It is true that we are who we are. It is also true that we can change who we are when we acknowledge our needs. The sinner's prayer begins with acknowledging our sinfulness. In the same way we must acknowledge the damaging thoughts and words that spew forth seemingly unprovoked.

There is hope and there is help when we turn to God. He is waiting for us to ask Him for help. It doesn't stop there. We need to make an effort to change what our eyes see and read, and what our ears are subjected to. We may also need to change our companions. We were not made into robots that blindly do as commanded. We were made into beings that think and make decisions.

Whenever we give up something, it must be replaced with a new action or reading material. A good place to start is with God's Word, the Bible. Find a translation you can read and understand. Then begin by memorizing the scripture so that it becomes part of our hearts. We will have the strength to withstand temptation because of what is within us. It is our decision!

What were you thinking?

> ".. Whatsoever things are true . . .think on these things."
> (Philippians 4:8 NJKV)

Several years ago, a power outage in Ontario and the U. S. caused major problems across our country. Airlines were in trouble as their computers; connected to the east were not sending and receiving accurate information. Accusations and innuendos flew back and forth across the international border. No one seemed to know for certain what caused the blackouts, but both countries were quick to point an accusing finger at each other. All we have at this point is speculation, and we may never know for sure what the problem was, or better yet, how it can be prevented from recurring.

As I listened to news reports I found a similarity between this situation and the way we tend to think. Frequently, our imaginations run away with us and we find ourselves imagining conversations in our minds that have very little basis in reality. That is, we hear of someone having difficulty. Only part of the story is actually heard and we begin constructing a possible scenario. There may be a minute grain of truth in our original musings, but the path of truth was left for a more interesting "bunny trail". Unfortunately, we may even go so far as to repeat our imaginings as a "prayer request" and thus the gossip mill has begun rolling.

The Bible says we are to think about, or dwell on, or meditate on, truth. Whatever the situation, we must ask ourselves whether the thoughts are thoughts of truth. Did the situation occur just as we think it did? Or have we added to it to make it look better or to justify our own sinful part in it? These are hard questions for us to answer. We must be tenacious in looking for truth, and these questions must be answered.

"... take captive every thought to make it obedient to Christ."

(2 Corinthians 10:5, NIV)

One unchangeable truth is that God loves us. We are accepted by Him – just the way we are. There is nothing we can ever do or say to help Him love us any more than He does now. Regardless of the situations we find ourselves in and the confusion that may occur, God is faithful and will never let us down. That's the truth!

The Wind

"Then he said to me, "Prophesy to the breath; prophesy, son of man, and say to it, 'This is what the Sovereign LORD says: Come from the four winds, O breath, and breathe into these slain, that they may live.'
"

(Ezekiel 37:9, NIV)

It wasn't raining when Noah built the Ark. Genesis 6 & 7 gives us the account of Noah building the ark. When it was completed, he and his family and the number of animals indicated by God entered the Ark. Then the rain started and it rained for 40 days and nights. It must have been quite a downpour! When the rain stopped, there was no land to be seen anywhere. In chapter 8 we are told that God sent a wind and the water receded. What really intrigued me about this story was the wind. God sent it. First, He caused the rain to fall until everyone and everything except for what was in the Ark was destroyed. The rain had come to put an end to the sin so rampant in that day. But God didn't stop at putting an end to everything. The water was God's judgment on sin. But then He sent a wind that caused the water to recede. He had a plan that blew away judgment and brought blessing.

The same still holds true today. God loves us and wants us to experience Him and be blessed by Him. The Holy Spirit may come as a gentle breeze, softly speaking to us in a still small voice, gently coaxing new life into our dried spirits, wooing us into action. The gentle breezes nurture tender plants. It is in these gentle times that God brings healing, comfort, and peace.

At other times He may feel like a gale force wind as the clutter and garbage is blown away, revealing underlying sin in our lives and re-enforcing our need of Him. A strong wind will uproot trees without a good root system in the same way the Holy Spirit will bring to light those things in our lives that have no basis in truth. Whatever the case, the wind of the Holy Spirit purifies as it blows the junk away, and His presence can be felt for a long time.

Come, Holy Spirit, we need you desperately! You are so powerful and strong. Help us destroy the wall surrounding our lives. We want you to remake our lives into people that are known by you. Please come Holy Spirit.

M. JOYCE HALVORSON

ISBN 142516059-X